World-Class Brain

AF147835

Harald S. Harung · Frederick Travis

World-Class Brain

The Edge that Helps Top Performers Succeed,
and How You can Develop It

Second Edition

 Springer

Harald S. Harung
Oslo, Norway

Frederick Travis
Fairfield, IA, USA

ISBN 978-3-031-86666-1   ISBN 978-3-031-86667-8   (eBook)
https://doi.org/10.1007/978-3-031-86667-8

1st edition: © Harald S. Harung and Frederick Travis 2018 2019
2nd edition: © The Editor(s) (if applicable) and The Author(s), under exclusive license to Springer
Nature Switzerland AG 2025

This work is subject to copyright. All rights are solely and exclusively licensed by the Publisher, whether
the whole or part of the material is concerned, specifically the rights of reprinting, reuse of illustrations,
recitation, broadcasting, reproduction on microfilms or in any other physical way, and transmission or
information storage and retrieval, electronic adaptation, computer software, or by similar or dissimilar
methodology now known or hereafter developed.
The use of general descriptive names, registered names, trademarks, service marks, etc. in this publication
does not imply, even in the absence of a specific statement, that such names are exempt from the relevant
protective laws and regulations and therefore free for general use.
The publisher, the authors and the editors are safe to assume that the advice and information in this book
are believed to be true and accurate at the date of publication. Neither the publisher nor the authors or
the editors give a warranty, expressed or implied, with respect to the material contained herein or for any
errors or omissions that may have been made. The publisher remains neutral with regard to jurisdictional
claims in published maps and institutional affiliations.

This Springer imprint is published by the registered company Springer Nature Switzerland AG
The registered company address is: Gewerbestrasse 11, 6330 Cham, Switzerland

If disposing of this product, please recycle the paper.

The purpose of this book is to contribute to higher performance and more happiness in the world

Preface

The brains of world-class performers are different from the brains of average performers. No surprise there. But what is surprising is that regardless of whether these top performers are athletes, musicians, or CEOs, their brains share one feature that makes them stand out: More integrated functioning. A world-class brain works in a more coherent, relaxed, wakeful, and efficient way.

World-Class Brain tells the story of these top performers and offers an easy-to-read introduction to the research showing that their brain function is different. This short book also describes other features that these top performers have in common, such as intensely happy and fulfilling peak experiences and a greater moral sense. Readers also learn how they, too, can effortlessly develop greater brain integration.

Oslo, Norway
Fairfield, USA

Harald S. Harung
Frederick Travis

Acknowledgments

The authors are grateful to Maharishi Mahesh Yogi—expert on higher human development—for making available the knowledge of the full range of human growth, and techniques to develop this potential in practice.

We are also grateful to Jim Karpen for all his inspiration and highly skilled assistance in preparing this book, to Morten Hvidsten, Ragnhild Boes, and Margot Suettmann for their many valuable contributions, to Gerry Geer and Fran Clark for proofreading the manuscript, and to Ferenc Csonti for preparing it for publication. Thanks also to Ken Daley, Susanne Cook-Greuter, Dennis Heaton, Yvonne Lagrosen, Niyazi Parim, and Anne Marte Pensgaard for helping with the research we report here.

Financial support has been provided by Maharishi International University, Oslo Metropolitan University, G. C. Rieber Funds, and Swedish Foundation for International Cooperation in Research and Higher Education.

Trademarks

Transcendental Meditation®, TM®, TM-Sidhi®, Maharishi Vedic®, and Maharishi International University are protected trademarks and are used in the US under license or with permission. The Performeasure® Assessment is the US trademark of Brain Integration Systems AS, Oslo, Norway.

Note on Terminology

This book integrates modern Western science and the ancient Vedic tradition of knowledge from India—as expounded today by Maharishi Mahesh Yogi as Maharishi Vedic® Science—to present a comprehensive picture of peak performance and human potential. Concepts from modern science include brain integration, peak experiences, moral reasoning, and ego or self-development. Concepts from Maharishi Vedic Science include Transcendental Consciousness, Unity Consciousness, higher states of consciousness, and collective consciousness. References to both types of concepts are given in the text.

Origin of Research Instruments and New Theories

Drs. Bob Cranson, Charles N. Alexander, Harald S. Harung, Ken Chandler, and Dennis Heaton conceived and developed the Survey of Peak Experiences; Dr. Fred Travis the Brain Integration Scale; Dr. Harald S. Harung the Unified Theory of Performance; and Dr. Harald S. Harung and Dr. Fred Travis the Performeasure Assessment.

Note from the Authors

This is a book about world-class performance. Since life and performance are multidisciplinary and holistic, so is this book. It involves many disciplines, including performance; brain, body, and genes; developmental psychology, including moral reasoning, motivation, and self-development; peak experiences and higher states of consciousness; leadership, management, and organizational behavior and development; sociology and societal development; practice, learning, and education; sports; music; computer programming; and quantum physics. To make this wide range of knowledge easily accessible to you, we have endeavored to present the knowledge in a simple and readable way.

Introduction by Harald S. Harung

Top athletes sometimes experience the "zone." In the midst of intense competition, time suddenly slows down or speeds up. Their performance becomes effortless, spontaneous, and of high quality. They feel deep inner happiness and connectedness. And they see everything with great clarity.

I had that experience years ago when I was performing at a high level in the sport of orienteering. It's challenging because not only do you need to run fast while having to deal with obstacles such as thick forests, fields of boulders, tall grass, and crags, but you also have to be fully alert as you use a map and compass to navigate and find the "control points"—small flags that have been placed to mark the course.

During a national race in my native Norway, I had a good feeling right from the start. Navigation was easy and running was effortless and joyful. Contrary to my normal experience, as the race progressed, I felt increasing exhilaration and energy. During the last uphill before the finish, I felt as if I was floating.

And I won the race.

I subsequently had the same experience of the zone in an even bigger competition: A three-day international orienteering race in Sweden. I had run good races during the first two days. I knew that if I performed at a satisfactory level on the third day, I would win the overall victory in my class.

During this third race, navigation was particularly effortless, almost automatic. I was alert, but restful at the same time. It was as if the control points were seeking me out—I had the good fortune to find them all quickly. Indeed, I was almost surprised when the last control suddenly appeared before my eyes.

And I won first place overall.

Some orienteering races have an added twist: They take place at night. This entails using a flashlight to see where you're going, to read the map and compass, and to spot the control flags. We were high up on a moor in the Lake District of northwest England. I felt good and strong—almost a feeling of invincibility.

Like my experience of the zone in earlier races, when the euphoria is there, both navigation and running are at a high level, and the race spontaneously unfolds in a natural way. All the diverse aspects of an orienteering race come together in a stellar performance, and you feel intense joy.

I won the British night orienteering championship and was named "Knight of the Night."

At that time, I had never heard about the zone or "peak experiences," as they are also called. I've never forgotten these profound experiences. Later I studied descriptions of other people having peak experiences and I wondered—what happens to the brain when you're in the zone? How is the brain different during peak experiences? Fortunately, as a university professor and having a top brain researcher as a colleague, I was able to find out.

That's what our book is about.

Harald S. Harung

Introduction by Frederick Travis

One afternoon in the late spring of 2008, Harald came into my office. I had just published two papers that reported research on individuals who had practiced *Transcendental Meditation*® for an average of 24 years and who were having experiences of higher stages of human development. Their experiences in some ways were similar to those of athletes in the zone: A feeling of connectedness with everything, extreme alertness, unboundedness, effortlessness, deep inner peace.

In my two studies, I had identified what was different about their brains. Simply put, their brains as a whole were more integrated, and I developed a scale to measure the level of integration.

Harald had recently published papers reporting elevated experiences in successful businesspeople, artists, writers, and scientists from 16 different countries. He wrote about their subjective experiences and wondered what was happening in their brains.

We shared our findings and discussed whether successful people might show the same pattern of brain integration that was seen in long-term practitioners of Transcendental Meditation.

We talked about how brain functioning underlies individual experience. For example, when you're tired, information flows more slowly between your brain's networks, especially the frontal executive brain areas—the CEO or boss of the brain. You lose the ability to see the big picture, to make plans, or to enjoy the positive side of your experience.

Higher brain integration means that individual brain areas are functioning together. You're able to place automatic emotional responses in context with past memories, and current plans and experiences. This ability is essential for successful performance in any area of life.

It would make sense, then, that high-level performers, whether athletes or managers or musicians, would show greater brain integration. And this might be the key to their excellent performance.

Harald and I decided to collaborate. We wanted to see how the brains of top performers differed from those of ordinary people.

That's what our book is about.

Frederick Travis

Contents

About the Authors

Dr. Harald S. Harung is an interdisciplinary researcher with a focus on peak performance and leadership, and a high performer in lecturing, writing, and the sport of orienteering. He holds a PhD from the University of Manchester and has worked as a researcher at Oxford University, naval officer, CEO of an engineering company, and president of an international business college. Harald was for many years teaching "Leadership, ethics, and world-class performance" to classes of up to 500 students at Oslo Metropolitan University. He has been working as a researcher and consultant on peak performance for more than 30 years, on both the individual and organizational level. Harald has published over 50 papers and five books, and lectures worldwide. To contact Dr. Harung and for further information, please visit www.harvest.no.

Dr. Frederick Travis has been Director of the Center for Brain, Consciousness, and Cognition at Maharishi International University since 1990. His work has focused on brain development from birth to adulthood, higher states of consciousness, and the effects of meditation experiences on the brain. Fred has published over 90 papers and four books. He teaches on the undergraduate, master's, and doctoral levels and lectures globally on brain and consciousness. The New York Academy of Sciences has invited Fred to present his research there. Fred and Harald together were the first researchers in the world to find a brain-basis of high performance, which forms a pillar of understanding excellence. To contact Dr. Travis, please visit www.drfredtravis.com or write to ftravis@miu.edu.

Abbreviations

EEG   Electroencephalography
fMRI   functional Magnetic Resonance Imaging
TM   Transcendental Meditation

List of Figures

List of Tables

Chapter 1
The Secret Revealed: Integrated Brain Functioning

Abstract This chapter starts our quest to answer the question: What underlies world-class performance? We cite research showing that age, work experience, education, practice, and incentives have only a small influence on performance. Instead, we found that the level of brain integration is key for high performance in diverse areas of life.

Everyone recognizes the genius of Albert Einstein, whose theory of relativity helped set off a revolution in physics. And everyone wants to have what he had: The capacity for peak performance. We all want to realize our fullest potential so we can be successful and happy. We want the sort of experience that Einstein described, an experience of the zone. Here's how Einstein talked about it[1]:

> There are moments when one feels free from one's own identification with human limitations and inadequacies. At such moments, one imagines that one stands on some spot of a small planet, gazing in amazement at the cold yet profoundly moving beauty of the eternal, the unfathomable: Life and death flow into one, and there is neither evolution nor destiny; only being.

What's different about these extraordinary people? We decided to find out by contacting world-class performers and arranging to assess their brains using electroencephalography (EEG). Brain functioning underlies behavior. So higher functioning people should have higher functioning brains. And this is what we found. Their brains functioned in a different way from that of most people.

But first let's demolish some common notions about the keys to peak performance. You might think it's age, work experience, education, practice, or incentives. It's none of these five factors. Let's take a look at some of the scientific findings.

---

[1] Martin & Ott (2013, p. 9).

© The Author(s), under exclusive license to Springer Nature Switzerland AG 2025
H. S. Harung and F. Travis, *World-Class Brain*,
https://doi.org/10.1007/978-3-031-86667-8_1

1

Does Age Explain Performance?

We see that age improves performance throughout childhood and adolescence. Many readers may think that age improves performance also in adults because we are accumulating more experience.

Researchers Frank Schmidt and John Hunter[2] of the US summarized thousands of studies spanning 85 years of research and involving millions of *adults* at work. They found that age was reported to have zero influence on level of performance. In other words, whether you are 25 or 45, your performance is basically at the same level. Researchers in the UK[3] later published another major meta-analysis that came to very similar conclusions.

Individuals reach their optimal level of performance in their early 20 s across different domains and this level continues throughout adult life. This may reflect the fact that our brain underlies thinking and acting, and that the brain grows through waves of natural maturation—programmed in our genes—from birth through the first 25 years of life.

Importantly, natural maturation interacts with ongoing experience that shapes and refines changes in brain connections. In principle one could continue to improve in performance throughout adult life by selecting experiences that facilitate further refinement of brain functioning. However, the research cited above found that work experience itself only explains 3% of the level of performance in adults. This could reflect the fact that most work performance simply strengthens current abilities and responses to challenges; it is not able to increase the level of brain integration.

But What About Education?

Unfortunately, the above researchers found that the number of years of education explained just 1% of performance in adults! They write that this is the correlation within the applicant pool of individuals who apply to get a particular job.

Education is of course essential for learning a profession. Education can enable you to get a more interesting job and is rewarding in itself. But why doesn't it contribute more to higher levels of performance? Current education focuses on facts, theories, and skills (e.g., computer or communication skills). Gaining intellectual knowledge by reading a book or taking a course, however interesting it may be, does not fundamentally refine our brain functioning. Rather, it increases connections within current brain areas. To achieve major shifts in our capacity for performance and happiness, a fundamental development of our brain and mind must take place. Unfortunately, this deeper transformation does not appear to result from our current intellect-based system of education.

---

[2] Schmidt & Hunter (1998).
[3] Robertson & Smith (2001).

Practice?

The benefits of practice for performance are supported by brain research at The Rockefeller University and UCLA published in Nature. The researchers used cutting-edge technology to observe 73,000 neurons in mice as they learned a task. The scientists found that repetitive practice solidifies neural pathways, transforming unstable memory representations into stable ones, leading to improved performance and mastery.[4]

So, how extensive are the benefits of practice for performance? It depends, writes Brooke Macnamara[5] who reviewed 88 studies of *deliberate practice* and performance in several activities. Deliberate practice is defined as engagement in structured activities created specifically to improve performance in a domain. According to Anders Ericsson,[6] who coined the term, deliberate practice consists of effortful repetition and hard work, beyond our comfort zone; well-defined, specific goals; full attention; and feedback and modifications of efforts in response to that feedback. He writes that expert performers develop their extraordinary abilities through a laborious process over many years and that there are no shortcuts. Ericsson concludes that deliberate practice will have much larger benefits for performance than the normal simple repetition of an activity.

But even for deliberate practice Macnamara found that the benefits are limited. In the repetitive performance of sports, deliberate practice explains about 18% of your level of performance, in music 21%, and in games 26%. This is because in repetitive activities practice is creating motor circuits in your brain to automatically guide performance. You don't need to think how you will respond. You just automatically swing the tennis racquet or jump over the high bar or play the same song on the piano as you have done thousands of times before.

But when it comes to knowledge-related work, such as computer programming or sales, practice explains less than 1% of the level of performance. In professional jobs, you need to constantly adjust your performance to the changing demands of the situation. You are not just habitually responding.

The averaged effect of deliberate practice across different activities was 12%. However, in a subsample of studies with a more rigorous assessment of performance, practice accounted on average for only 5% of the variance in performance. Macnamara concludes:

> The deliberate practice view is an important and influential theoretical account of expert performance, but the claim that individual differences in performance can largely be accounted for by deliberate practice is not supported by the available empirical evidence.

The conclusion about the limitations of practice to reach world-class performance is strengthened by a second study led by Macnamara.[7] This study analyzed 52 data

---

[4] Bellafard et al. (2024)

[5] Macnamara et al. (2014).

[6] Ericsson & Pool (2016).

[7] Macnamara et al. (2016).

sets on the relationship between deliberate practice and performance in high-level sports. In this study, practice accounted for just 1% of the performance differences among elite athletes (national and international level). She concludes:

> While practice is necessary for elite athletes to reach a high level of competition, after a certain point, the amount of practice essentially stops differentiating who makes it far and who makes it to the very top.

Practice does not make perfect. There is a saying "practice makes perfect." However, it is more accurate to say that "practice makes permanent." Repeating a task over and over builds habitual patterns of brain functioning and behavior. The "practice makes perfect" saying was appropriate in earlier times when simple, manual work dominated in society—like carpentry, shoemaking, and baking. Today, with increasing levels of complexity, automation, and speed of change, more and more work is becoming knowledge work. Each situation is a new situation that requires careful analysis. This is why practice is reported to have almost zero effect on the performance of knowledge work. Thus, as time goes by, practice will contribute less and less to top performance.

Incentives?

There is another myth about peak performance. Namely, if you want people to improve their performance, give them an incentive, usually money. However, the role of incentives in performance depends on the type of work. If you're building a wall, incentives can help drive performance. But if you're building a company or performing other knowledge work, incentives can actually be detrimental.[8] Again, with the ongoing shift from simple manual work to more sophisticated knowledge work, we need to fundamentally rethink what motivates people to do a good job. A lot of money may in fact decrease inner motivation, the key to world-class performance.

Let's give a few examples of how high performers tend to be *intrinsically* motivated (driven by a search for meaning, happiness, passion, and competing against oneself), and not *extrinsically* motivated (winning, money, fame, power, and competing against others).

Think of Steve Jobs, founder of Apple, when he returned to save the company he once founded and worked for $1 per year, without receiving any shares or options.[9] His motivation was making computers personal and putting his company back on the fast track, not making money for himself.

In sports, Ole Einar Bjørndalen, often known as "The King of Biathlon," is the most successful ski sport athlete of all time, having won a total of 58 medals in the Olympic Games and world championships, the last in 2017 at the age of 43.

---

[8] Kohn (1999).

[9] Town (2007).

According to an article[10] titled "Medals don't mean anything," Ole Einar said that he doesn't collect medals; he collects good races.

During the 2018 Olympic Games in Pyeongchang, South Korea, the cross-country skier Marit Bjørgen became the most-winning winter Olympian of all times with eight gold medals, four silver, and three bronze—a total of 15 medals. She indicates that she isn't driven by money when she notes[11]:

> What am I going to do with 4 or 12 million dollars? It won't give me a better life anyway.

Genes?

Another factor that may explain performance level is our genetic makeup. A review of the research literature[12] found that genetically influenced factors may make an important contribution to performance level in music and sport. For instance, the number of fast-twitch muscles—which are important in many sports—appears to be genetically determined and does not increase with physical practice.[13] However, this doesn't mean that if we aren't born with specific innate abilities we should just give up. It's better, we believe, to accept one's genetic endowment and seek to refine functioning in our chosen arena. In addition, we believe one should focus on developing one's mind and brain—in order to express the *universal potential* we all share.

Integrated Brain Functioning is Key

The key to peak performance, we have found in our research, is integrated brain functioning, as measured by EEG. What this means is that the top-performing brain is more coherent. The various parts of the brain, each of which has different responsibilities, are collaborating in a better way—like the musicians of an orchestra working in concert. The brain is more relaxed and wakeful, and more efficient (using less energy to perform a task). Fred[14] has combined these three different measures into his *Brain Integration Scale* (see later for more details of this scale).

In our research, world-class performers in sports and business scored substantially higher on this scale than controls. Thirty-three world-class athletes had higher levels

---

[10] Haugli (2010).

[11] Nesje (2014).

[12] Macnamara et al. (2016).

[13] Suwa et al. (1996).

[14] Travis et al. (2002).

of brain integration compared to 33 average athletes.[15] And 20 top-level managers had greater brain integration compared to 20 low-level managers.[16]

The results from our study of classical musicians were unexpected. We found that the 25 professional classical musicians had high levels of brain integration, but the brain integration scores of the 25 amateur classical musicians were almost as high.[17] This could have resulted from the fact that if you play music from childhood, which both the professional and amateur musicians had, your brain is more integrated as an adult (see Chapter 7). Also, the distinction between professional and amateur musician does not necessarily distinguish musical ability. Rather, it distinguishes how a person makes his or her livelihood.

We also measured moral reasoning and frequency of peak experiences in the top performers and their average-performing controls. We added the scores on brain integration, moral reasoning, and peak experiences to give a comprehensive measure of mind-brain development. As we shall see, we found that the high-performing athletes, managers, and musicians *all* scored much higher on mind-brain development than did their controls.

* * *

Brain integration is key. Fortunately, there are practical methods to foster continuous improvement in brain functioning throughout life, as we shall see in Chapter 7 in this book. We think that such growth will have profound benefits for education, individual life, organizations, and society.

In this book, you'll meet some of the world-class athletes, managers, and musicians who took part in our research. You'll hear about their careers, their successes, and their inspiring descriptions of peak experiences during optimal performance. You'll also learn exactly what it means to enhance the level of integrated brain functioning.

And we'll go even further, discussing how short-lived peak experiences, which many of us enjoy once or twice in a lifetime without knowing how to trigger them, can become lasting. For some people, this subjective experience isn't spontaneous and intermittent; rather, it's the ongoing reality of everyday life. Fortunately, we all have the potential for such a highly rewarding life.

And finally, we'll present research that shows individuals with integrated brains create more integrated societies.

With the ongoing shift from manual to knowledge work, the increasing tempo of life, and the increasing application of artificial intelligence, higher mind-brain development is becoming increasingly important for high levels of performance and happiness in individuals and in society—and for a sustainable and peaceful world.

---

[15] Harung et al. (2009/2011).

[16] Harung & Travis (2012).

[17] Travis et al. (2011).

References

Bellafard, A., Namvar, G., Kao, J. C., Vaziri, A., & Golshani, P. (2024). Volatile working memory representations crystallize with practice. *Nature, 629*, 1109–1117. https://neurosciencenews.com/crystallized-memory-practice-26135/. Retrieved July 28, 2024.

Ericsson, A., & Pool, R. (2016). *Peak: Secrets from the new science of expertise.* Houghton Mifflin Harcourt Publishing Company.

Harung, H., Travis, F., Pensgaard, A. M., Boes, R., Cook-Greuter, S., & Daley, K. (2009). Higher psycho-physiological refinement in world-class Norwegian athletes: Brain measures of performance capacity. *Scandinavian Journal of Medicine and Science in Sports, 21*(1), 32–41. Published online in 2009 and in print in 2011.

Harung, H. S., & Travis, F. T. (2012). Higher mind-brain development in successful leaders: Testing a unified theory of performance. *Cognitive Processing, 13*, 171–181.

Haugli, K. B. M. (2010, February 19). Medaljer betyr ingenting (Medals don't mean anything). *Aftenposten.*

Kohn, A. (1999). *Punished by rewards: The trouble with gold stars, incentive plans, A's, praise, and other bribes.* Houghton Mifflin.

Macnamara, B. N., Hambrick, D. Z., & Oswald, F. L. (2014). Deliberate practice and performance in music, games, sports, education, and professions: A meta-analysis. *Psychological Science, 25*(8), 1608–1618.

Macnamara, B. N., Moreau, D., & Hambrick, D. Z. (2016). The relationship between deliberate practice and performance in sports: A meta-analysis. *Perspectives on Psychological Science, 11*(3), 333–350.

Martin, W., & Ott, M. (2013). *The cosmic view of Albert Einstein.* Sterling Publishing.

Nesje, E. (2014, November 28). Bjørgen: Hva skal jeg med 30 eller 90 millioner? Jeg får ikke noe bedre liv likevel (What am I going to do with 4 or 12 million dollars? It won't give me a better life anyway). *Aftenposten.*

Robertson, I., & Smith, J. (2001). Personnel selection. *Journal of Occupational and Organizational Psychology, 74*, 441–472.

Schmidt, F., & Hunter, J. (1998). The validity and utility of selection methods in personnel psychology: Practical and theoretical implications of 85 years of research findings. *Psychological Bulletin, 124*, 216–274.

Suwa, M., Nakamura, T., & Katsuta, S. (1996, August). Heredity of muscle fiber composition and correlated response of the synergistic muscle in rats. *American Journal of Physiology, 271*(2 Pt 2), R432–6.

Town, P. (2007). *Rule #1: The simple strategy for successful investing in only 15 minutes a week!* Three River Press.

Travis, F., Tecce, J., Arenander, A., & Wallace, R. K. (2002). Patterns of EEG coherence, power, and contingent negative variation characterize the integration of transcendental and waking states. *Biological Psychology, 61*, 293–319.

Travis, F., Harung, H. S., & Lagrosen, Y. (2011). Moral development, peak experiences and brain patterns in professional and amateur classical musicians: Support for a Unified Theory of Performance. *Consciousness and Cognition, 20*, 1256–1264.

Chapter 2
Brain Integration in World-Class Athletes

Abstract We tested the brains of world-class athletes and average-performing controls using EEG. We found that the world-class athletes had much more coherent, relaxed, wakeful, and efficient brain functioning.

As we noted earlier, we were eager to see whether there were differences in the brains of top performers compared to those less accomplished. Our first impulse was to study athletes.[1] This was an obvious choice, because the level of performance in athletes is readily evident from their success in competition. We could compare the top performers to control athletes who were matched in terms of gender, age, type of sport, and level of education but who had been less successful during competition. We chose elite athletes connected to the National Olympic Training Center and the Norwegian School of Sport Sciences in Harald's native Norway. We'll call them "Olympic athletes" since most of them had performed at a high level in the Olympic Games.

Fred packed the EEG amplifier and sensors into a camera bag and headed for the airport in Cedar Rapids, Iowa, USA. The Transportation Security Administration officials took a long time examining the amplifier. Finally, after inspecting it carefully and checking for any trace chemicals, they let Fred and the amplifier onto the plane. Fourteen hours later he was landing in the Gardermoen airport in Oslo.

Meanwhile, Harald had met with the National Olympic Training Center and the Norwegian School of Sport Sciences. Working together, they selected 59 athletes who for at least three seasons had placed among the top 10 in major competitions like the Olympic Games, world championships, or World Cup. Of these, 33 agreed to be part of the study. They had competed within the last five years and were at least 25 years old. They came from endurance sports such as cross-country skiing, orienteering, the biathlon, and long-distance running; technical sports such as downhill skiing, shooting, and offshore boat racing; and team sports such as soccer and handball.

Together they had won a large number of medals at the Olympic Games, world championships, and European championships: 175 gold medals, 108 silver, and 78

---

[1] Harung et al. (2009/2011).

© The Author(s), under exclusive license to Springer Nature Switzerland AG 2025
H. S. Harung and F. Travis, *World-Class Brain*,
https://doi.org/10.1007/978-3-031-86667-8_2

bronze. This is a total of 361 medals, which means an average of about 11 medals per top athlete. Additionally, in first place finishes in World Cup competitions, they had a total of 321 victories, an average of about 10 per athlete. In total, they had an average of about 20 top finishes in major international competitions. They really were world-class.

These top athletes were compared to a control group of athletes who had been active in training and competing at the senior level for at least three seasons but did not normally place amongst the top 50% in the Norwegian championships.

Harald had also arranged with Oslo Metropolitan University to reserve an office for the research. It took two hours to transform the office into an EEG lab, with a table for the athlete to take an assessment via a laptop computer and to fill out forms, and with the EEG amplifier to the side. The testing included not only EEG measurements but also some standardized psychological assessments as well as a structured interview. Altogether, it would take a couple of hours.

Mind-Brain Testing Procedure

Thomas Alsgaard was among the first subjects Fred tested. He had won a total of 11 gold medals in the Olympic Games and world championships, making him one of the world's most successful cross-country skiers ever. Tall, strong, and handsome, with dark hair and deep-set eyes, Thomas came ready to be plugged in. He explained that his own experience, and his observation of many other top performers, suggests that these athletes often don't perform at top level during training and preparation. However, when it comes to major championships, they excel and may even appear to perform above their abilities. He found that the peak experiences we describe seem to cover well this tendency to excel when it matters most. Thomas was fascinated by the idea that there could be a neurophysiological basis of such exceptional performance, and for this reason he wanted to be tested in our research.

The first step was signing a consent form. Next came the EEG measurements, which were the easiest part. Fred uses technology that features a colorful cap with 32 holes to add sensors. Fred put the cap on Thomas's head and then began the 20-min process of applying the 32 sensors for the EEG measurements. The cap is connected to a laptop computer that records the subject's brain waves—the tiny electrical pulses associated with *neurons* (brain cells) firing. Once the sensors have been attached, the software runs a test to see if all the sensors are in place.

Not one to waste time, Fred asked Thomas to fill out the psychology assessments during the process of attaching the sensors. Then once the sensors were attached and Thomas had arrived at a natural stopping point in the psychological testing, Fred had him start on the EEG testing.

This testing itself took less than 20 min, as Thomas sat at the computer and played a very simple game with two parts.

The first part, a simple reaction time task, took three minutes. It involved an asterisk appearing on the screen followed by a tone 1.5 s later. Fred gave him a game-controller-like button for his right hand and asked him to press it as soon as he heard the tone.

The second part, a choice reaction time task, also took three minutes. This task involved a one- or two-digit number flashing on the screen followed by a second one- or two-digit number 1.5 s later. Thomas pressed a left- or right-hand button on the game-controller indicating which number was bigger.

The objective of the reaction time test was to see how the brain would prepare to respond during the two tasks.

Brain Coherence

What's the value of brain wave coherence? Coherence means that the different parts of the brain—which carry out different tasks—are working more in synchrony and harmony with each other. It is like a well-functioning business, where the different departments—such as production, sales, marketing, and accounting—are communicating and collaborating in a good way.

In our research we calculated EEG left and right frontal coherence during the two choice reaction time tasks described above. The frontal area of the brain is like the CEO of a company. It receives information from other parts of the brain and integrates it, and then it activates the rest of the brain in a coordinated way. When there's more coherence in the prefrontal cortex, it's better able to unite perception, planning, strategizing, and behavior into more successful performance.

An athlete like Thomas, we hypothesized, must have high frontal coherence. Imagine all that's involved in cross-country skiing. Every moment one has to attend to a range of stimuli and react accordingly. Changing conditions include competitors; bends in the track; whether the terrain is uphill, flat, or downhill; the air temperature; and the quality of the snow (new, old, soft, hard, wet, dry, coarse, or fine-grained). And it must happen nearly instantaneously since there's no time to think.

As anticipated, we found that the top performers in sports had high frontal coherence.[2]

Later on, other researchers have provided support for our hypothesis that brain coherence provides the basis for high performance. First, EEG coherence in the right hemisphere is positively related to ethical and inspirational/charismatic leadership.[3] Second, higher coherence between EEG signals from the left and right sides of the frontal cortex is associated with higher creativity.[4] Third, brain functional connectivity—which gives a similar picture to coherence—was a robust predictor of

---

[2] Harung et al. (2009/2011).

[3] Waldman et al., (2011, 2016).

[4] Lustenberger et al. (2015).

individual creative ability.[5] Fourth, a study[6] in Australia concluded that greater brain connectivity is associated with higher intelligence scores.

The most convincing support for our theory comes from a major study by Professor Stephen Smith[7] at Oxford University and his co-workers. This study used fMRI—functional Magnetic Resonance Imaging—which measures blood flow patterns inside the brain. They compared connectivity between 200 locations with 280 different psychological and behavioral measures recorded for the same persons. According to the researchers, those with high brain connectivity scored higher on measures typically deemed to be positive, such as vocabulary, memory, and life satisfaction. They also had higher income and more years of education. In contrast, those with low brain connectivity exhibited high scores for traits typically considered negative, such as anger, rule-breaking, substance use, and poor sleep quality.

Alpha1 Brain Waves and Relaxed Wakefulness

The purpose of the reaction time task was to see how each athlete's brain functioned when she or he was challenged. We had hypothesized that not only would we see coherence in his brain during these tasks, but also that his brain would be more relaxed and wakeful, and more efficient.

Specifically, we hypothesized that he would have greater alpha1 (brain waves at 8–10 cycles per second) amplitude or power[8] in his brain waves along with lower gamma amplitude or power. Alpha1 power is an indicator of restful brain activity. Think about it: Typically, the athlete who performs best is the one who is the calmest, who has greater presence of mind in frantic situations. He or she isn't distracted by the pressure or the chaos but instead is more inner-directed. That's an indication of alpha1 power. When a person gets caught up in a situation and loses this calm and restful mindset, then the brain typically is dominated by higher gamma power (see Chapter 6).

Given Thomas's stature as a world-class athlete, we expected that he would have this mindset of a top performer—and that we'd measure higher alpha1 power and lower gamma power in the frontal and central areas of his brain. Indeed, that's what we found in Thomas and, in general, in the other top performers.

The peak performers are calm and alert at the same time. That enables them to be most adaptable to changes in the environment, such as changes in the behavior of teammates or the opposition.

---

[5] Beaty et al. (2018).

[6] Hearne et al. (2016).

[7] Smith et al. (2015).

[8] See Chapter 6 for a definition of power.

The importance of alpha1 brain waves for athletic performance is supported by research[9] showing that high alpha1 brain wave power correlates with efficiency of movement and economy of effort in top performers.

Efficiency of Brain Functioning

In addition to brain wave coherence in the prefrontal cortex, and the relative strength of alpha1 and gamma brain waves over the whole brain, we also looked at a measure of efficiency of Thomas's brain functioning. We measured this by looking at the brain's "preparatory response." In both computer tasks that Thomas engaged in, there was an initial stimulus and then a second one.

We looked at what his brain did between the first and second stimulus in both tasks. We simply wanted to see when the brain got active. For example, in the second task, would his brain get active as soon as he saw the first number in anticipation of the second number? Or would it wait until he had the necessary information from the second number to make an accurate response?

As we hypothesized, Thomas activated more brain resources before the simple reaction time task since there was only one possible response. In contrast, he remained balanced with reduced mobilization during the choice task while he waited for the second stimulus before he started to respond. Notice this style of response is most appropriate for both tasks.

We found the same efficiency of brain function in the other top athletes.

But what about the control group? The brain preparatory responses of the control subjects were the opposite. They actually had reduced brain preparatory response during the simple task and heightened brain preparatory response during the choice task. Simply put, the brains of the world-class athletes were more efficient since they matched better the changing conditions of different tasks.

Brain Integration Scale

These three brain measures are combined to form the *Brain Integration Scale*: Coherence in the frontal cortex, higher alpha1 power along with lower gamma power, and more appropriate brain preparatory response. This scale is a convenient way of coming up with a *single* number that represents the level of a person's brain development.

The Brain Integration Scale has been a real boon to our research, because having a single number makes it easier to compare groups and to assess brain development in a range of professions. And so far, our research suggests that the key to high levels

---

[9] Hatfield et al. (2004).

of performance is having an integrated brain. Clearly, Thomas and other top athletes have brain wave signatures that distinguish them from the less successful athletes.

The difference between the top and average athletes was supported by an additional measure that reflects efficiency of bodily functioning: How fast the athletes stopped responding—how quickly they habituated—to an irrelevant sound or noise. The world-class athletes habituated about three times faster than the average-performing athletes. This indicates that the top performers were better able to ignore distractions and focus on what was important for success.

* * *

Once the EEG testing was done, Fred had Thomas finish up the psychological assessments.[10] In less than two hours, Fred had gotten the measures that would give him a good indication of Thomas' brain function, his psychological profile, and his familiarity with peak experiences.

Over the next three weeks, Fred recorded EEG from 33 world-class athletes and 33 control athletes. For the next four months, he looked at the data and selected periods of EEG that were clear and not affected by the person moving during the tasks. After analyzing those data, we found that our hypothesis was supported—that top athletes had higher levels of brain integration. Their brains were more integrated and efficient. We were then eager to look at top performers in a different profession: Management.

References

Beaty, R. E., Kenett, Y. N., Christensen, A. P., Rosenberg, M. D., Benedek, M., Chen, Q., Fink, A., Qiu, J., Kwapil, T. R., Kane, M. J., & Silvia, P. J. (2018). Robust prediction of individual creative ability from brain functional connectivity. *Proceedings of the National Academy of Sciences of the United States of America, 115*(5), 1087–1092. Epub 2018, January 16.

Harung, H., Travis, F., Pensgaard, A. M., Boes, R., Cook-Greuter, S., & Daley, K. (2009). Higher psycho-physiological refinement in world-class Norwegian athletes: Brain measures of performance capacity. *Scandinavian Journal of Medicine and Science in Sports, 21*(1), 32–41. Published online in 2009 and in print in 2011.

Harung, H. S., & Travis, F. (2016). *Excellence through mind-brain development: The secrets of world-class performers.* Routledge.

Hatfield, B., Haufler, A., Hung, T.-S., & Spalding, T. (2004). Electroencephalographic studies of skilled psychomotor performance. *Journal of Clinical Neurophysiology, 21*, 144–156.

Hearne, L. J., Mattingly, J. B., & Cocchi, L. (2016, August 26). Functional brain networks related to individual differences in human intelligence at rest | Semantic Scholar. *Nature, Scientific Reports.* https://www.semanticscholar.org/paper/Functional-brain-networks-related-to-indivi dual-in-Hearne-Mattingley/30a8188cd49efc5e75edcfd198af1135475d5bfa#:~:text=It%20is% 20found%20that%20greater%20connectivity%20in%20the,to%20encompass%20more%20c omplex%20and%20context-specific%20network%20dynamics. Retrieved October 12, 2024.

---

[10] Harung & Travis (2016).

Lustenberger, C., Boyle, M. R., Foulser, A. A., Mellin, J. M., & Fröhlich, F. (2015, June). Functional role of frontal alpha oscillations in creativity. *Cortex, 67*, 74–82. https://doi.org/10.1016/j.cortex.2015.03.012. *Epub* 2015, April 1.

Smith, S. M., Nichols, T. E., Vidaurre, D., Winkler, A. M., & Behrens, T. E. J. (2015). A positive-negative mode of population covariation links brain connectivity, demographics and behavior. *Nature Neuroscience, 18*, 1565–67.

Waldman, D. A., Balthazard, P. A., & Peterson, S. (2011). The neuroscience of leadership: Can we revolutionize the way that leaders are identified and developed? *Academy of Management Perspectives, 25*(1), 60–74.

Waldman, D., Wang, D., Hannah, S. T., & Balthazard, P. (2016). A neurological and ideological perspective of ethical leadership. *Academy of Management Journal, 59*, 5.

Chapter 3
Brain Integration and Moral Development in Top Managers

Abstract We tested top-level managers in the private and public sector and compared them to low-level managers. We found that the top managers scored significantly higher than the controls on brain integration and moral reasoning.

Introduction

Athletes live in a world in which their every performance is minutely measured. They're accustomed to being tested, analyzed, and assessed in every possible way. Their whole focus is peak performance.

Managers also strive to perform on a high level. However, the business environment is not as clearly defined as a sports event and so managerial success is not as easily measured. The ability of the manager's company to make money is one indication of the manager's performance. But other factors are also crucial, such as the ability of managers to inspire associates, their stability in the workplace, their values and integrity, and their broad vision for their company and its role in the larger world.

Selecting the Top Managers

We had some choices to make here. We realized we didn't simply want to select managers who were effective at making money for their organization, because sometimes they do so by manipulating people, not paying a fair wage, causing fear, or not contributing their fair share to the community. Money is easy to measure but it does not necessarily reflect high levels of leadership. So instead, we decided to select top managers using quantitative and qualitative criteria other than money. We wanted to involve those who had shown successful leadership for 10 or more years,

© The Author(s), under exclusive license to Springer Nature Switzerland AG 2025
H. S. Harung and F. Travis, *World-Class Brain*,
https://doi.org/10.1007/978-3-031-86667-8_3

who were exemplary individuals, and who had a broader perspective than just maximizing profit. We wanted managers with a sense for sustainability and corporate social responsibility.[1]

Of course, finding top managers for our study wasn't quite as straightforward as contacting Norway's National Olympic Training Center. But Harald had an idea: Contact someone in his native Norway who for decades had taken a keen interest in Norwegian leadership in practice. That individual turned out to be Tor Dahl, who had been the CEO of a major staffing and selection company in the Nordic countries and Europe for more than 35 years.

The company Tor formerly headed, Manpower Europe and Norway, was a pioneer in value-based management, i.e., management based on sound human values such as equality, trust, moral values, and self-managing associates. An example of a core value that guided Tor's management was, "We believe that people are trustworthy and seek meaning through their work." Under his leadership, Manpower became the largest staffing company in Norway.

Tor found our testing of brain integration and moral reasoning to be innovative and important—innovative because brain testing adds a new perspective to performance assessment and important because having sound moral values is becoming increasingly important in a complex and rapidly changing world where more and more people are making independent decisions.

Since Norway is a small country, it was relatively easy for Tor to have a sense for which managers in this country were really tops. He identified 38 top-level managers. We contacted them, and 20 agreed to take part in the study. They had held their positions for an average of about 18 years. Sixteen were from the private sector and four from the public sector. Among the 16 in the private sector, nine were successful entrepreneurs, and seven led companies that were publicly traded. A final check of the list was provided by Magne Lerø, the editor of the Norwegian weekly management magazine *Ledelse*.

Brain Integration in the Top-Level Managers

We compared the group of top managers to a control group of individuals who were similar with regard to age, gender, level of education, and type of organization, but who had limited managerial responsibility. Most were low-level managers, such as project managers, senior engineers, or product managers. A few were skilled knowledge workers.

It is unusual for managers to have their EEG measured. Helping to coordinate the research on the managers was Morten Hvidsten, who marveled at how bold we were. Imagine a brain researcher going into companies and top executives sitting down to have their brain waves recorded while they viewed a computer screen and pressed buttons. Morten said:

---

[1] Harung et al. (2009), Harung & Travis (2012).

To make it easy for subjects to participate in the study, Fred brought his portable EEG equipment to several different locations. As he was setting up his equipment at a large corporation in Oslo, we were attracting attention from curious office workers. And I thought to myself, "How amazing — some of these business executives are actually having their brains scanned, right in the middle of their workplace."

The testing for managers was the same as that for athletes: Taking EEG readings while the subjects performed tasks on a computer screen, as well as pencil-and-paper psychological assessments.

As with the athletes, the top managers had significantly higher scores on the Brain Integration Scale compared to the control group.[2] Their leadership, their effectiveness, and their broad vision were accompanied by more coherent brain function, more alpha1 power or amplitude, and more appropriate brain preparatory responses.

Why would that be? We suspect that higher levels of brain integration could lead to more integrated and effective perception, planning, and action. Managers are always in the challenging situation of having to focus on details while also at the same time needing to maintain the big picture. They have to keep the broad strategy in mind while also adopting specific tactics to meet their objective.

Also, more alpha1 power means more wakefulness and broad awareness. Wakefulness and broader awareness are important for a manager to be creative and to recognize new opportunities.

The capacity for CEOs to make effective decisions has a further brain correlate, as shown by researchers at Wake Forest University.[3] This study concluded that the most successful leaders have more gray matter in brain areas that control decision-making and memory, thus giving them a vital edge when it comes to making the right decisions.

Moral Reasoning in the Top-Level Performers

Yet there may be even one more benefit of an integrated brain that's more important than those mentioned so far. If, as our research suggests, a top-level manager with an integrated brain has broader vision that goes beyond the day-to-day minutiae, perhaps that vision would extend to an appreciation for the ethics of one's actions. Ideally, a top-level manager would not only be effective and successful in the workplace but would also ensure that the behavior of the company was ethical—and would take into account the impact on others, society, and the environment.

This topic of moral development has been of interest to researchers, and it's been found that some people are a cut above: They have a higher level of psychological development than the norm. Researchers have created standardized assessments to measure a person's level of psychological development.

---

[2] Harung & Travis (2009, 2012).

[3] Hannah et al. (2013).

So far, general intelligence has dominated as a psychological measure of performance capacity since it correlates well with level of performance.[4] However, general intelligence has been found to have a very low correlation with integrity.[5] This suggests that a performer with high intelligence could be involved in both ethical *and* unethical activities.

For simplicity we wanted to use only one measure of psychological development. Thus, since more and more people are making independent decisions, we decided to measure moral reasoning instead of general intelligence.

Gibbs's socio-moral reasoning questionnaire presents moral statements and asks subjects to describe why a moral act may be important to them. For example, it asks subjects to complete the statements: "Keeping promises is important because ..." and "Helping one's friend is important because ...".

Findings for managers. Interestingly, we found that the top-level managers had higher levels of moral reasoning than their controls. And their moral reasoning scores correlated with their higher levels of brain integration.

Higher moral reasoning means that they have a broader perspective when they act, thinking not only of themselves but also of others, their society, and even the whole world.

Did these findings surprise us? Yes, we're saying that top managers, according to our research, tended to have higher moral values than low-level managers. This is quite the opposite of conventional wisdom, which often characterizes business executives as immoral. Research[6] has for example found that 80% of Americans do not trust corporate executives and—worse—that roughly half of all managers do not trust their own executives.

However, we selected those top managers who showed genuine leadership according to our qualitative criteria. That's because our research is focused on optimal human development—what characterizes it and how it can be developed. As we noted above, making money isn't necessarily an indicator of genuine high performance. There can be many ways to make money, many of which are not ethical.

Finally, compared to many other countries, the business climate may be different in Norway, a country that is characterized by trust and equality. In fact, in all the Nordic countries (Denmark, Finland, Iceland, Norway, and Sweden), social segregation is much smaller and social mobility much higher than in for example the US, write Wilkinson and Pickett[7] in *The Spirit Level: Why Equality Is Better For Everyone*. These same authors[8] conclude, "The more equally wealth is distributed the better the health of that society." This claim is supported by the 2023 *World Happiness Report*,[9] where all five Nordic countries were listed amongst the seven happiest nations in the world.

---

[4] Schmidt & Hunter (1998).

[5] Ibid.

[6] Hurley (2006).

[7] Wilkinson & Pickett (2010).

[8] Pickett & Wilkinson (2009).

[9] World Happiness Report (2023).

Findings for athletes. We also found that the top athletes as a group scored significantly higher than the average-performing controls on moral reasoning. In contrast, there have been several studies[10] reporting low levels of moral reasoning in professional athletes in the US. Why might there be a discrepancy between our study and these other studies?

Norwegian Olympic athletes may have a very different motivation to compete than US professional athletes. Simply put, US pro athletes make large amounts of money. In contrast, Norwegian Olympic athletes earn much less money, and their goal may be a purer desire for peak performance, self-expression, and happiness. They may have been more intrinsically motivated.

We studied primarily athletes who participated in individual competition, whereas the US studies looked at team sports. Also, our subjects were at least 25 years old, which wasn't the case with the US studies. This is relevant because research has shown that one's brain and moral development aren't fully mature until one is approaching the age of 25. Finally, the level of pro-social behavior is higher in Norway than in the US, suggesting a higher level of ethics in the Scandinavian country.

Another objection we have encountered is that the athletes around the world who have been found to use performance enhancing drugs to perform at a high level are not examples of high levels of moral reasoning. We of course agree. These athletes may have a high-level performance for a short time but it is not accompanied with feelings of expansion, ease, and effortlessness. Also, these athletes will burn out very quickly. Thus, they are not *genuine* peak performers. They therefore support our finding that there is a correlation between level of moral reasoning and level of performance.

Mind-Brain Profile

We are confident that a mind-brain profile of peak performers is emerging from our research. They are successful because their brains function in a more integrated way, and in practice that translates into improvements in thinking and behavior, such as a tendency to appreciate the broader moral implications of one's actions. It's not surprising that this would be the case, since our EEG research shows greater integration in the frontal areas of the brains of top performers. These same frontal areas of the brain have been shown to be active during moral reasoning tasks. Fred's research also directly shows that high brain integration correlates not only with greater moral reasoning but also with higher emotional stability, more openness to experience, and lower anxiety[11] and with greater creativity.[12]

---

[10] See for example: Long et al. (2006).

[11] Travis et al. (2004).

[12] Travis & Lagrosen (2014).

Recall that we found a similar result in our study of world-class athletes. They not only showed greater brain integration compared to controls, but they also scored higher on the Gibbs assessment of moral reasoning, and there was a positive correlation between these two measures.

* * *

Thus, our research strongly suggests that high performance is associated with higher brain integration and that this again is correlated with higher levels of moral development.

The next step in our research was to examine a third category of top performers to see if we'd get similar results. We felt this would help us further consolidate our profile of peak performers. We chose classical musicians. As you'll see in the next chapter, this group in particular helped us to gain insight into what it truly means to be a peak performer.

References

Hannah, S., Balthazard, P., Waldman, D. A., Jennings, P. L., & Thatcher, R. W. (2013). The psychological and neurological bases of leader self-complexity and effects on adaptive decision-making. *Journal of Applied Psychology, 98*(3), 393–411.

Harung, H. S., & Travis, F. T. (2012). Higher mind-brain development in successful leaders: Testing a Unified Theory of Performance. *Cognitive Processing, 13*, 171–181.

Harung, H. S., Travis, F., Blank, W., & Heaton, D. P. (2009). Higher development, brain integration, and excellence in leadership. *Management Decision, 47*(6), 872–894.

Hurley, R. F. (2006). The decision to trust. *Harvard Business Review, 84*(9), 55–62.

Long, T., & Pantale´on, N., Bruant, G., & d'Arripe-Longueville, F. A. (2006). Qualitative study of moral reasoning of young elite athletes. *Sport Psychology, 20*, 330–347.

Pickett, K. E., & Wilkinson, R. G. (2009). Greater equality and better health. *BMJ, 339.* https://doi.org/10.1136/bmj.b4320

Schmidt, F., & Hunter, J. (1998). The validity and utility of selection methods in personnel psychology: Practical and theoretical implications of 85 years of research findings. *Psychological Bulletin, 124*, 216–274.

Travis, F., & Lagrosen, Y. (2014). Creativity and brain-functioning in product development engineers: A canonical correlation analysis. *Creativity Research Journal, 26*(2), 239–243.

Travis, F., Arenander, A., & DuBois, D. (2004). Psychological and physiological characteristics of a proposed object-referral/self-referral continuum of self-awareness. *Consciousness and Cognition, 13*(2), 401–420.

Wilkinson, R. G., & Pickett, K. (2010). *The Spirit Level: Why Equality is Better for Everyone.* Penguin Books, United Kingdom.

World Happiness Report 2023 | The World Happiness Report. Retrieved November 13, 2023.

Chapter 4
Brain Integration and Peak Experiences of Musicians

Abstract We tested professional classical musicians in major orchestras in Norway and Sweden and compared them to amateur classical musicians. We found that the professional musicians scored significantly higher than the amateurs on moral reasoning and frequency of peak experiences, but that the level of brain integration was similar in both groups. However, the professional musicians scored higher on several other brain-related measures.

Having found higher levels of brain integration in world-class athletes and top managers, we then turned to classical musicians. There's now a body of research showing a special relationship between playing music and brain development. Learning to play an instrument is an excellent way to develop greater cognitive ability.

We were eager to see if top professional classical musicians had higher levels of brain integration than amateur classical musicians.

For the musicians the selection criteria were straightforward: We compared professionals and amateurs. Thus, we tested 25 musicians who were permanently employed by the Oslo Philharmonic Orchestra, the Norwegian Opera in Oslo, and Gothenburg Symphony Orchestra in Sweden; and 25 musicians who played in various amateur symphony orchestras in Oslo and the surrounding county of Akershus, and in Gothenburg. The two groups were matched for age, gender, and level of education.

The amateur musicians were employed in a variety of professions, including business and management, IT-consulting, education, engineering, geology, research, pharmacy, nursing, and interior design. Both groups had been playing their instruments since they were around five years old.

Like managers, musicians aren't accustomed to being tested, and it's not always easy to recruit subjects. But Harald had a plan. He would give presentations to the orchestras and take along a shower cap. During the presentation, he'd take out the shower cap and put it on his head to show them what it would be like to have the EEG cap on. Of course, they found it amusing, and they agreed to participate. We got the subjects we needed.

© The Author(s), under exclusive license to Springer Nature Switzerland AG 2025
H. S. Harung and F. Travis, *World-Class Brain*,
https://doi.org/10.1007/978-3-031-86667-8_4

The testing proceeded as before: Placement of the EEG cap and electrodes, and psychological assessments. We had hypothesized that the professional musicians would have higher levels of brain integration compared to the control group of amateur musicians. Indeed, the professional musicians did score high on the Brain Integration Scale—but so did the amateur musicians.[1]

Brain Integration

It was a surprise to us that the amateur musicians had levels of brain integration that were very similar to the professional musicians: 2.48 for the professionals compared to 2.45 for the amateurs. This was on the same level as that of the world-class athletes (2.5) and top managers (2.48), and significantly higher than for the control athletes and managers—1.3 and 1.54 respectively.

At first, we weren't sure what to think, but then we realized that it's quite possible that a lifelong pursuit of musical performance is simply good for the brain and develops brain integration irrespective of whether one is amateur or professional.

Research has shown that children playing music enhances their visual-spatial, verbal, and mathematical performance as adults. For example, an fMRI study by researchers[2] at McGill University in Canada reported that 15 months of musical training in early childhood changed the brain structure of the participants when they were adults. Specific areas of the brain showing greater refinement in participants compared to controls were those areas involved in controlling hand motion, processing sounds, and coordinating both sides of the body.

The Canadian study may explain why the brains of both musician groups in our study were finely tuned. Also, we realized that the amateur musicians, in some cases, may have been as accomplished as the professionals but were amateurs more or less by choice, having chosen to focus on a career in a different profession. They very well may have been performing at a similarly top level in their chosen profession.

However, we did indeed find a difference in brain function on several other measures. The professional musicians scored higher in tests involving faster resolution of perceptual conflict, higher vigilance levels, and a tendency for faster speed of brain processing. Plus, the professional musicians also scored significantly higher on the assessment of moral reasoning discussed previously. This suggests that although their brain integration is similar to that of the amateurs, these top musicians do have an edge in other mind-brain areas.

---

[1] Travis et al. (2011).

[2] Schlaug et al. (2005).

Peak Experiences

But in what was the most important assessment, the professional musicians really stood out: The frequency of peak experiences. For us, this is key. It's one thing to be a top performer in one's profession, but it's even better if one's subjective experience is similar to the experiences that Harald wrote about in the introduction to this book. Peak experiences are moments of optimum human development and happiness—this is when one is living the full value of life. One's awareness is greatly expanded, which is very different from one's normal waking experience. And happiness is high as illustrated by research showing that peak experiences are the best predictor of well-being.[3] This is, we feel, the most important point we have to make: It's possible to live life at a more exalted level.

Consider, for example, an experience of intense happiness or euphoria, which is perhaps the most rewarding aspect of being in the zone. The professional pianist Gonzalo Moreno[4] from the Oslo Philharmonic Orchestra noted:

> … an incredible feeling of euphoria. I feel like the happiest person in the world.

This is an example of an experience that's well beyond the norm. We hypothesized that these peak experiences are the result of higher levels of brain integration, and that top performers would have them more frequently.

We measured peak experiences with a questionnaire called *Survey of Peak Experiences.*[5] The survey asked about the frequency of four categories of peak experiences:

1. During rest or relaxation.
2. During activity.
3. During sleep.
4. Luck.

To illustrate this survey, here is Question 1, which pertains to peak experiences during resting or relaxation with eyes closed:

> During practice of relaxation, meditation, prayer, or any other technique — or when you have relaxed or had a quiet moment — have you then experienced a completely peaceful state, a state when the mind is very awake, but quiet, a state when consciousness seems to be expanded beyond the limitations of thought, beyond the limitations of time and space?

And here is Question 2, which asks for a peak experience during activity:

> Have you experienced that while performing activity there was an even state of silence within you, underlying and coexisting with activity, yet untouched by activity? This could be experienced as detached witnessing even while acting with intense focus.

---

[3] Poloma & Pendleton (1991).

[4] Harung & Travis, (2016, p. 15).

[5] Harung et al. (1996).

Table 4.1 Frequency of subjects reporting at least one peak experience in life

(Percentage)	World-class	Controls
Athletes	73	71
Managers	91	82
Musicians	100	80

The top performers scored higher than the controls in all three professions, but only the managers and musicians showed significant differences

The purpose of these questions is to bring out the experience of transcendence.[6] Transcendence is a distinct state of awareness that lies beyond even the most refined mental activity (see Chapters 8 and 9). The term *peak experience* was coined by Abraham Maslow,[7] who related it to transcendence, the most fundamental, most blissful, and most expanded mental level. As might be expected, in our research the replies to the Survey of Peak Experiences questionnaire seem to include both genuine experiences of transcendence as well as normal waking experiences of deeper mental levels, but not as deep as transcendence. During scoring we excluded peak experiences that we considered not to be genuine.

Table 4.1 summarizes the percentage of persons—world-class performers and controls—who reported at least one peak experience in their life.

Our research on frequency of peak experiences can be summarized as follows:

- Although our world-class athletes reported a wide range of peak experiences,[8] the frequency of such glimpses was not significantly higher than for their controls.
- The top-level managers had significantly more frequent peaks during rest or relaxation (Question 1) and there was a trend for greater luck (Question 4).
- The professional musicians reported significantly more peak experiences during rest or relaxation, activity, and sleep (Questions 1, 2, and 3).

Findings for musicians. As seen in the table, the professional musicians scored highest of all our subject groups on this survey—100% of them reported at least one such experience in life. Even more impressive, though, was that the professional musicians had more of a tendency to experience all four of the categories of peak experiences that we asked about. The average total number of times they reported having experienced all four categories was 17.4, which was substantially higher than 10 for the amateurs.

Clearly, the professional musicians were having profound experiences. What were these experiences like? A piano soloist[9] with the Oslo Philharmonic Orchestra narrates his experience this way:

---

[6] We did not use the word transcendence in the questionnaire since this term may not be familiar to some people.

[7] Maslow (1968, pp. 105, 113).

[8] Harung (2012).

[9] Travis et al. (2011).

> It is difficult to describe, but it feels like experiencing a kind of eternity, contrary to everyday life, which is in continuous movement.

The cellist Johannes Martens[10] from the Oslo Philharmonic Orchestra explained that after their best performances he felt an:

> … intense feeling of happiness and meaningfulness.

Findings for managers and athletes. Subjects in our other two studies also reported peak experiences.[11] The top managers reported significantly more incidents than their controls of peak experiences during eyes closed rest or relaxation (Question 1), and a trend for greater luck (Question 4). Here is an experience of good luck reported by one of the top executives we studied[12]:

> It seems to me that I often have luck in business, when buying a property or something. It often turns out that those business options that did not come through would not have been so smart. However, I would have chosen these business options if something outside my control had not come in the way.

The handball goal keeper Heidi Tjugum[13] was a member of the Norwegian national team that won many medals: One gold and one silver in world championships, one silver and one bronze in Olympic Games, and one gold and two silver in European championships. She was also part of the club team that won two European Cups. Heidi said:

> I have quite a lot of times experienced a state where I am completely inside myself and everything else disappears. This is a form of relaxation. … And there is nothing that can touch me. It feels very good. It is not that those periods are so very long. But it is beautiful to have them, once a week or once a day.

Heidi said that everything felt right and there was nothing that could disturb her. She enjoyed an expanded awareness and said that after many years she can still remember a large number of details of her best matches: The lights in the sports hall, the colors of the clothing worn by the spectators, and all the different smells.

Why do the musicians have more peak experiences than the athletes? There are two complementary types of happiness. First, object-dependent happiness occurs when we satisfy some outer need or aspiration, e.g., buying a new house or winning a sport competition. This happiness tends to be temporary. Second, there is a self-referral happiness where one is happy without any particular reason. As one becomes more and more familiar with transcendence, this inner happiness increases until it culminates in permanent inner bliss when one is fully established in transcendence[14] (see also Chapter 9). Of the two, inner happiness is the most important because of its high intensity and lasting nature.

---

[10] Harung & Travis (2016, p. 15).

[11] Harung (2012).

[12] Harung & Travis (2016, p. 70).

[13] Harung (2012).

[14] Maharishi ([1963] 2001, 1969).

Music stimulates inner happiness by enlivening the deepest mental levels of feelings and transcendence. This stimulation can take place in many of the musicians during large portions of the music and tends to trigger peak experiences. In contrast to music, sports are more directed toward achieving an outer goal, and there often is substantial strenuous activity before the outer goal is reached, usually at the end of the competition. The happiness that results therefore tends to be more object-dependent and is often limited to those who do best, and peak moments are triggered less frequently. However, due to their pronounced contrast with the strenuous activity, peaks that do occur in sports may be experienced as having high intensity. This contrast may explain why peak experiences often receive more attention in sports than in music.

Overall, our research shows that more integrated brain functioning is reflected in more integrated inner experiences. One's sense of self is more expanded and more settled, and one is happier within. This provides a stable inner foundation for making difficult decisions. With this inner contact, the top performers could depend more on their deep feelings and intuition. This is a practical result of higher brain integration. You are more in tune with your inner hunches and intuition.

Previous Studies on Peak Experiences and High Performance

The importance of peak experiences for world-class performance is supported by a pilot study that Harald[15] carried out before we researched the athletes, managers, and musicians. The subjects in the pilot study were people known internationally for their ability to achieve and maintain a position among the top performers in their areas of activity, such as business, government, sports, education, and the performing arts.

These 22 high achievers came from 16 countries from around the world. We assessed their frequency of peak experiences and compared them to students who had responded to the same questions. There was a significant difference between the two groups on two categories of peak experiences—transcendence during resting/relaxation (Question 1) and during sleep (Question 3).

The wide range of professions in our pilot study suggests that peak experiences aren't unique to the three professions—athletes, managers, and musicians—that we subsequently studied. In other words, high achievers in any field will tend to have peak experiences and likely also would score high on the Brain Integration Scale.

Similarly, studies by other researchers have found peak experiences in a variety of activities. Research[16] on athletes has reported a wide range of peak experiences during optimal performance. And a study[17] of mostly historic, truly world-class performers in a wide range of activities found that they often reported profound

---

[15] Harung et al. (1996), Harung (1999/2018).

[16] See for example: Jackson & Csíkszentmihályi (1999).

[17] Pearson (2013).

peak experiences. Those reporting a comprehensive range of rewarding moments include athletes such as Pelé (soccer), Billie Jean King (tennis), and Roger Bannister (running); poets such as Emily Brontë and Walt Whitman; scientists such as Maxwell and Schrödinger; composers such as Beethoven and Mozart; and national leaders such as Vaclav Havel (Czech Republic) and Anwar el-Sadat (Egypt).

Flow. Flow is another rewarding inner experience that is connected to improved performance. Flow might be considered a more general experience—and a lesser experience—compared to a peak experience. With humor, flow can therefore be called a "peak experience light." Flow is simply the experience of performance triggered by a match between challenge and ability,[18] while genuine peak experiences are based on transcendence, as just seen. Peaks therefore belong to the upper range of flow experiences.[19]

Based only on subjective descriptions it is unavoidable that sometimes the two concepts are mixed. But when we turn to the objective measurements done by for example EEG, the distinction between flow and peak experiences is readily evident, as was brought out by a recent study at the University of Skövde in Sweden. This study found that the brain characteristics of flow were those of waking consciousness[20] as clearly opposed to the brain features of transcendence.

A 2024 neuroimaging study at Drexel University's Creativity Research Laboratory in the US unveils how the brain enters the creative flow state. Using EEG to analyze jazz improvisations, the researchers John Kounios and David Rosen found that flow combines extensive experience with a conscious release of control. This "expertise-plus-release" model suggests that deep creative flow is more accessible to those with significant experience and the ability to let go.[21]

Our research on world-class performers suggests that the ability to let go increases even more during a peak experience as compared to flow. As seen, orienteering is a complex sport where one in a forest runs as fast as possible while using a map and a compass to find one's way to several marked check points. Bjørnar Valstad, who won four world championships and one World Cup in orienteering, recollects that when he won the 2004 world championship classical distance, he enjoyed such a high degree of automation in action that we can use the word "witnessing" to describe it[22]:

> I feel quite safe in some way … And all the things I'm doing are in some way just sitting in the background. Mentally, in orienteering we have map-reading, but it's going automatic … When I'm in this mode, there are no negative thoughts. It's like sitting in a car with an autopilot and just sitting watching. I notice something happen in front of me and I need to do something and then back again, and you just sit there. When [in] the race, this is quite simple. It's getting to know how to practice this, which is most difficult.

---

[18] Csíkszentmihályi (1975, 1991).

[19] Jackson & Csíkszentmihályi (1999, p. 13).

[20] Andersson (2022).

[21] Kounios & Rosen (2024).

[22] Harung & Travis (2016, p. 67).

Even through flow is not as rewarding as peaks, a longitudinal study carried out by McKinsey[23] found that productivity increased five times when top executives experienced flow. The German management consultants Fabritius and Hagemann[24] describe an interesting observation regarding skill level and the frequency of flow, an observation which is similar to our own findings on world-class performance and frequency of peak experiences:

> It's important to note that your chances of experiencing flow increase in proportion to your abilities. The higher your skill level, the more likely the occurrence of flow.

* * *

These peak experiences of expanded awareness and intense happiness get to the heart of our book. We feel this is how life should be lived. Based on these studies and other research, we contend that everyone can develop higher levels of brain integration, everyone can enjoy peak experiences, and everyone can experience greater success. In fact, we'll go so far as to say that it's possible to experience a state when these peak experiences are an ongoing reality rather than a fleeting occurrence.

At the root of a peak experience is a coherent, relaxed, wakeful, and efficient brain—in short, a more integrated brain.

References

Andersson, I. (2022). Brain activity during flow: A systematic review. https://www.diva-portal.org/smash/get/diva2:1687530/FULLTEXT01.pdf. Retrieved December 1, 2023.

Csíkszentmihályi, M. (1975). *Beyond boredom and anxiety.* Jossey Bass.

Csíkszentmihályi, M. (1991). *Flow: The psychology of optimal experience.* Harper.

Fabritius, F., & Hagemann, H. W. (2017). *The leading brain: Powerful science-based strategies for achieving peak performance.* A TarcherPerigee Book.

Harung, H. S., Heaton, D. P., Graff, W. W., & Alexander, C. N. (1996). Peak performance and higher states of consciousness: A study of world-class performers. *Journal of Managerial Psychology, 11*(4), 3–23.

Harung, H. S. (2012). Illustrations of peak experiences during optimal performance in world-class performers: Integrating Eastern and Western insights. *Journal of Human Values, 18*(1), 33–52.

Harung, H. S., & Travis, F. (2016). *Excellence through mind-brain development: The secrets of world-class performers.* Routledge.

Harung, H. S. (1999/2018). *Invincible leadership: Building peak performance organizations by harnessing the unlimited power of consciousness.* MIU Press. Original printed version can be ordered from www.miupress.org. Updated 2018 eBook version on www.amazon.com.

Jackson, S. A., & Csíkszentmihályi, M. (1999). *Flow in sports: The keys to optimal experiences and performance.* Human Kinetics.

Kotler, S. (2014). *The rise of superman: Decoding the science of ultimate human performance.* Amazon Publishing.

Kounios, J., & Rosen, D. (2024). https://neurosciencenews.com/creativity-zone-neuroscience-25697/. Retrieved March 11, 2024.

---

[23] Kotler (2014, Chapter 1).

[24] Fabritius & Hagemann (2017, p. 111).

Maharishi Mahesh Yogi. ([1963] 2001). *Science of being and art of living: Transcendental meditation*. Revised and updated edition. Plume (a member of Penguin Putnam).

Maharishi Mahesh Yogi. (1969). *On the Bhagavad-Gita: A new translation and commentary*, Chapters 1–6. Penguin.

Maslow, A. H. (1968). *Toward a psychology of being* (2nd ed.). Van Nostrand Reinhold.

Pearson, C. (2013). *The supreme awakening: Experiences of enlightenment throughout time—and how you can cultivate them*. MIU Press. www.miupress.org.

Poloma, M. M., & Pendleton, B. F. (1991). *Exploring neglected dimensions of religion in quality of life research*. Edwin Mellon Press.

Schlaug, G., Norton, A., Overy, K., & Winner, E. (2005). Effects of music training on the child's brain and cognitive development. *Annals of New York Academy of Science, 1060*, 219–230.

Travis, F., Harung, H. S., & Lagrosen, Y. (2011). Moral development, peak experiences and brain patterns in professional and amateur classical musicians: Support for a unified theory of performance. *Consciousness and Cognition, 20*, 1256–1264.

Chapter 5
A Single Value Underlying Performance

Abstract We combined the three measures of brain integration, moral reasoning, and frequency of peak experiences into a single variable that we called the Performeasure® Assessment. For this combined measure there was a substantial difference between the world-class performers and the controls for all three studies that we carried out.

While there were certainly differences between the study group and control group in our three studies, this difference wasn't always as large as we had hypothesized, i.e., peak experiences in athletes and brain integration in musicians. But what if we combined all three measures into a single measure? What would be the contrast then?

We did just that—and found a marked and highly significant difference between the study group and control group for the athletes, managers, and musicians. We refer to this single measure as the Performeasure Assessment.[1]

Previous research has concluded that a combination of several psychological factors like general intelligence, personality, interests, and integrity can predict up to 50% of performance.[2] Adding physiological measures, such as brain integration, and subjective experiences, such as peak experiences, could further improve the predictive power.

The Performeasure Assessment

Table 5.1 shows the Performeasure Assessment for the three studies, with standard deviations in parentheses. The relatively low standard deviations suggest that the Performeasure Assessment accounts for most of the differences between the groups. As seen, there is a highly significant difference between the high and average

---

[1] Harung & Travis (2016, Chapter 6).

[2] Schmidt & Hunter (1998), Martin (2014).

© The Author(s), under exclusive license to Springer Nature Switzerland AG 2025
H. S. Harung and F. Travis, *World-Class Brain*,
https://doi.org/10.1007/978-3-031-86667-8_5

Table 5.1 Mean values and standard deviations (in parentheses) for the Performeasure Assessment for the world-class performers and controls for the athletes, managers, and musicians

Profession	World-class performers (standard deviation)	Controls (standard deviation)	Statistical significance
Athletes (n = 33)	2.77 (1.59)	0.80 (1.29)	p < 0.0001
Managers (n = 20)	4.26 (1.10)	2.68 (1.54)	p < 0.001
Musicians (n = 25)	4.84 (0.45)	3.45 (1.21)	p < 0.001

The table shows that there is a substantial difference in scores on mind-brain development between the peak and average performers for all three studies

performers even though the number of people in each group is relatively small, ranging from 20 to 33.

Benefits of a Single Number

Recall our finding that on almost all of the nine measures of brain integration, moral reasoning, and frequency of peak experiences for our three studies, the high performers scored significantly higher than the controls—the only exceptions being the frequency of peak experiences for the athletes and the brain integration for the musicians. But when we add the three measures together, we get a highly significant difference for all three studies, as shown in the table. Thus, the advantage of a single, combined number is that it is more *robust*.

Also, the single Performeasure number allows the large differences between the high and average performers to be seen more clearly. Figure 5.1 summarizes the results of the Performeasure Assessment from the three studies to further illustrate the substantial difference between the top and average performers. As seen, overall, the top performers scored almost twice as high as the controls. The p-value shown suggests that there is 1 chance in 1000 that the difference between the two groups is a coincidence.

* * *

This chapter has provided a comprehensive picture of what underlies high performance and happiness. Of the three dimensions we examined, we think that brain integration is key. In the next chapter we'll therefore explain brain integration in more detail. You'll learn more about the parts of the brain and what it means to say that they are functioning more coherently. The important point is that this is objective science. Differences in brain function have been identified, and these differences are associated with optimum performance and extraordinary subjective experiences. We strongly feel that everyone should know about this research and about this possibility for greater human potential and bliss.

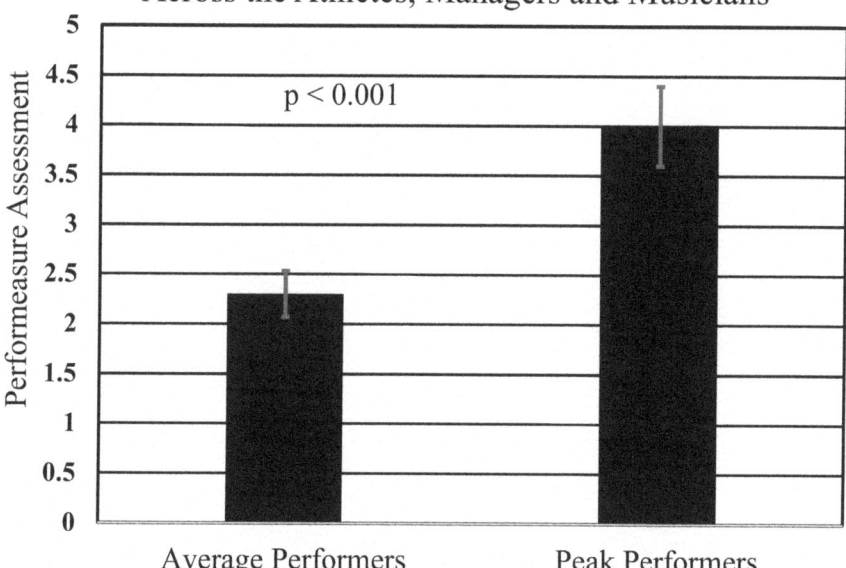

Fig. 5.1 The Performeasure Assessment scores averaged across the athletes, managers, and musicians (The figure compares the sum of the scores on mind-brain development for all the top performers to that of all the controls in our three studies)

Then in Chapter 7, we'll go into detail on how *you* can develop greater brain integration. Chapter 8 takes a closer look at Transcendental Meditation—an effective method to facilitate mind-brain development. Next, Chapter 9 introduces higher states of consciousness, which is development beyond the three commonly known states of consciousness: Waking, dreaming, and sleeping.

References

Harung, H. S., & Travis, F. (2016). *Excellence through mind-brain development: The secrets of world-class performers.* Routledge.

Martin, W. (2014, August 27). The problem with using personality tests for hiring. *Harvard Business Review.* Based on an address given by Frank L. Schmidt on Nov. 6, 2013, to Personnel Testing Counsel Metropolitan Washington Chapter.

Schmidt, F., & Hunter, J. (1998). The validity and utility of selection methods in personnel psychology: Practical and theoretical implications of 85 years of research findings. *Psychological Bulletin, 124,* 216–274.

Chapter 6
Understanding the Details of Integrated Brain Functioning

Abstract We introduce the amazing complexity and potential of the human brain and describe two ways to measure brain activity—Electroencephalography (EEG) and functional Magnetic Resonance Imaging (fMRI). Brain coherence, power, and efficiency—as measured by EEG—is then examined in detail.

Our three studies on peak performers show that these individuals all have the same characteristic brain patterns, and that these patterns are also associated with broader moral awareness and the sort of elevated experiences that are often reported by accomplished musicians, successful leaders, top athletes, and others performing on a high level.

Let's look in more detail at what's different about their brains. As we discussed in Chapter 2, the secret is brain integration, which has three components: Coherence in the frontal cortex, higher alpha1 power and lower gamma power over the whole brain, and a more efficient brain preparatory response.

Complexity of the Human Brain

By understanding brain complexity you'll have a greater appreciation of the scientific basis for the hypothesis that developing brain integration can lead to better performance. And you'll have a better understanding of the validity of the various means for developing brain integration that we'll discuss in the next two chapters.

We'll begin with the most basic component of the brain: *Neurons.* Your brain has approximately 100 billion of them, and all your feeling, thinking, perception, and behavior emanates from the functioning of these neurons. Table 6.1 below illustrates the amazing complexity of your brain.

In addition to the neurons, there are ten times as many *glial* cells. The neurons "fire" or transmit electrical impulses to each other, and this activity can be measured. In contrast, the glial cells are silent, but they are critical for the firing of neurons. There are two types of glial cells. One type ensures the brain has the energy it needs;

© The Author(s), under exclusive license to Springer Nature Switzerland AG 2025
H. S. Harung and F. Travis, *World-Class Brain*,
https://doi.org/10.1007/978-3-031-86667-8_6

Table 6.1 Amazingly complex human brain

1	Over 100 billion neurons or brain cells
2	More than 1,000,000,000,000,000 connections among the neurons
3	Takes more than 30 million years to count all connections (assuming it takes 1 s to count each connection)
4	Number of possible signal paths in the brain is larger than the number of elementary particles in the whole universe[1]

The numbers above illustrate the immense complexity and potential of the human brain

they maintain the *synapses* or gaps where one neuron talks to another; and they help in repairing the brain during sleep. The second type wraps around the axons that connect different neurons, and this speeds up the flow of information between neurons. This is a glimpse of the immense complexity of the human brain.

Structure of the Brain

Over the past century, scientists have come to know quite a lot about the various structures of the brain and their purposes. For example, the brain has a vertical structure. The outer layers of the *cortex*[2] are primarily involved in rational thinking and language (see Fig. 6.1). The next inner structure, the *limbic* system, is involved with emotions and memory. And the inner-most structure of the brain—the *reptilian* area—is more involved with instinctual responses, such as the survival instinct. Intuition results from the interplay of emotions and instinct.

Also, the brain has a back-to-front structure. The back of the brain processes sensory input and creates a picture of the world. The front part of the brain reflects on the picture of the world created in the back of the brain. The front of the brain takes the present and puts it in relation to the past and future. The front part of the brain plans and executes complex tasks. It is responsible for moral reasoning and sense of self. The frontal lobes are the executive areas of the brain—or as already noted, the CEO—that coordinate all the other brain areas.

Neuroscience can identify brain areas involved in different tasks and so discriminate brain patterns underlying thinking processes. These brain patterns can be measured in various ways. The firing of neurons can be measured using electroencephalography (EEG). Blood flow can be measured using functional Magnetic Resonance Imaging (fMRI). There are other ways to image the brain, but we'll focus on these two in greater detail.

---

[1] Storm (2014).

[2] Also known as the *neocortex*.

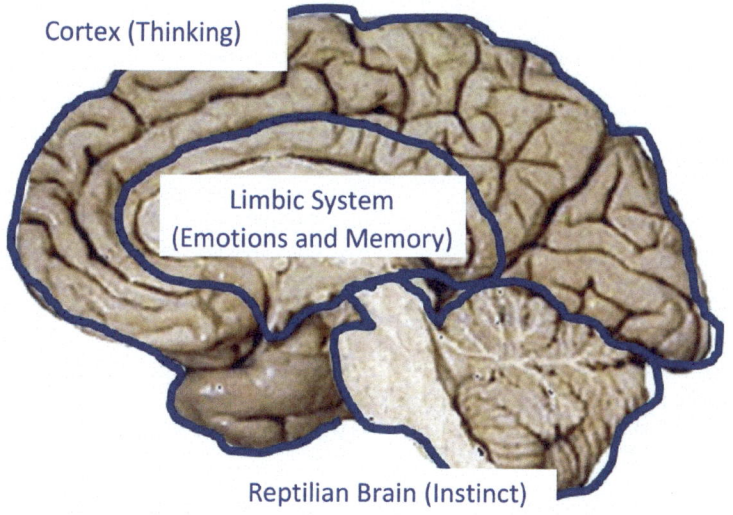

Cortex (Thinking)

Limbic System (Emotions and Memory)

Reptilian Brain (Instinct)

Fig. 6.1 The vertical structure of the brain (The figure shows three major vertical structures of the brain: Cortex [thinking], limbic system [emotions and memory], and reptilian brain [instinct])[3]

Two Ways to Measure Brain Activity

Electroencephalography—EEG. In 1924 in Germany, Hans Berger placed two large sensors on his son's head: One on his forehead and one on the back of his head. Berger fed the difference between the two electrical signals into a primitive oscilloscope and saw an 8–12 Hz wave when his son's eyes were closed and a 16–25 Hz wave when his son's eyes were open (Hz stands for Hertz and means cycles per second: How many peaks you see in the wave every second). Berger named the first wave he saw "alpha," the first letter of the Greek alphabet, and the second wave he saw "beta," the second letter of the Greek alphabet. These names—quite arbitrary—are still used today.

EEG measurement gives an excellent picture of millisecond-by-millisecond changes in the electrical state of the brain under each sensor on the scalp. Because the sensors sit on the scalp, the activity from a 2-cm (almost 1 inch) diameter of brain tissue is recorded by each sensor. Normally there are 32 sensors. All the brain activation in that 2-cm circle adds up to what is recorded at the sensor. Thus, EEG is sensitive time wise, but not space wise. More about this later.

Each brain wave frequency band is associated with a specific type of cognitive processing. Table 6.2[4] presents the EEG frequencies referred to in this book and the cognitive processes they are associated with. Notice that the slowest brain waves,

---

[3] Holden (1979).

[4] Adapted from: Travis (2012, pp. 66–68).

Table 6.2 EEG frequencies and cognitive processes

Brain wave type	Frequency (cycles/sec or Hz)	Cognitive processes
Delta	1–4	Restoration during sleep
Theta	5–8	Following inner mental processes such as during a memory task
Alpha1	8–10	Relaxed wakefulness, inner-directed attention
Alpha2	10–12	Brain primed to be used, but currently quiet
Sigma	12–16	The marker of sleep onset
Beta	16–20	Focus or concentration
Gamma	20–50	Strong focus or concentration

Brain activity underlies the activity of our mind. The table shows the brain's various frequency bands in cycles per second—as referred to in this book—and the corresponding cognitive processes

delta, are seen during deep sleep—when the brain is being restored. The fastest brain waves are called gamma waves and are seen during strong focus or concentration.

The electrodes can only tell you what's happening on the surface of a brain. It's sort of like putting an ear (or 32 ears) to the roof of a domed football stadium. You can hear the crowd cheering, yet you have little knowledge of the specifics of the game. However, the loudness of the cheers, their frequency, and the side of the stadium that they're coming from could give you a good idea of what's going on.

Similarly, an EEG sensor can tell you how often the neurons are firing (frequency) and, in a sense, how loud they are (amplitude). This works because individual neurons next to each other work together. So their activity sums up and can be measured on the scalp.

The photo in Fig. 6.2 shows Fred at work in the Center for Brain, Consciousness, and Cognition. Notice the stretch cap with the wires from the 32 sensors being fed into the amplifier—the small box to the right in the photo.

Functional Magnetic Resonance Imaging—fMRI

The fMRI technology images blood hemoglobin when it is oxygenated or deoxygenated. While being able to pinpoint what is going on within 2–3 mm areas of activation, fMRI works very slowly—it needs 3 s or longer to respond. Plus, the subject needs to lie down on a narrow bed in a small shaft in a scanner—it is too claustrophobic for many people.

Pros and cons. Each recording technique has its pros and cons. Fred likes EEG because the amplifiers are relatively inexpensive and quite portable, and the EEG can be easily recorded and analyzed on a laptop. In contrast, fMRI measurements require a shielded room and a million-dollar piece of equipment. EEG also has better time resolution (thousandths of a second) compared to fMRI (3 s or longer).

Fig. 6.2 The brain center at Maharishi International University in the US (The photo shows Fred applying sensors in preparation to record the EEG)

This is important when you are investigating moment-by-moment changes in inner experience. Large brain areas work together when processing information, so the poor spatial resolution of EEG (2 cm) is tolerable. The value of EEG measurement is reflected in its extensive use in clinical and research applications.

Analysis of the Brain Waves

Coherence. Earlier we discussed EEG coherence. Coherence gives a picture of the regions of the brain that are working together. In terms of our football stadium analogy, it's as if the cheers from the crowd start happening in synchrony from various parts of the stadium. That indicates that those fans are involved in the same cheering. Similarly, when two different brain areas are working together on the same task, then their brain waves will be more coherent.

The illustration in Fig. 6.3 shows the coherence between various areas of the frontal cortex in a typical low-level manager compared to a typical top-level manager, taken from our research. A line between two points signifies that the electrical brain waves at these points are at least 70% coherent with each other. A thicker line indicates even greater coherence. High coherence in the frontal part of the brain, as shown here, suggests that all aspects of the brain's executive center—the CEO—are working together.

Power. A second measure from the EEG analysis that we so far have not discussed in detail is how high the EEG wave is, i.e., its amplitude. If there are more neurons under the electrode that are oscillating in step with each other at the same frequency, then the EEG amplitude in that frequency will be higher. Squaring the amplitude, we get the *power* of the brain wave for each electrode.

The frequency with the highest power in the world-class performers was alpha1. This frequency indicates that their awareness is awake and alert; they are more centered, calm, and alert at the same time. Higher alpha1 amplitude in the world-class performers allowed them to not get too caught up in the heat of performance. Instead, higher alpha1 power was the brain pattern that indicated that the subjects remain more balanced and present, being able to focus intently while maintaining an inner calm.

Efficiency. The third component of the Brain Integration Scale is the brain's preparatory response. In this case we were simply looking at the brain waves to see exactly when the brain became more active during the computer task, and how active it got. As we described in detail in Chapter 2, the brain preparatory response of top

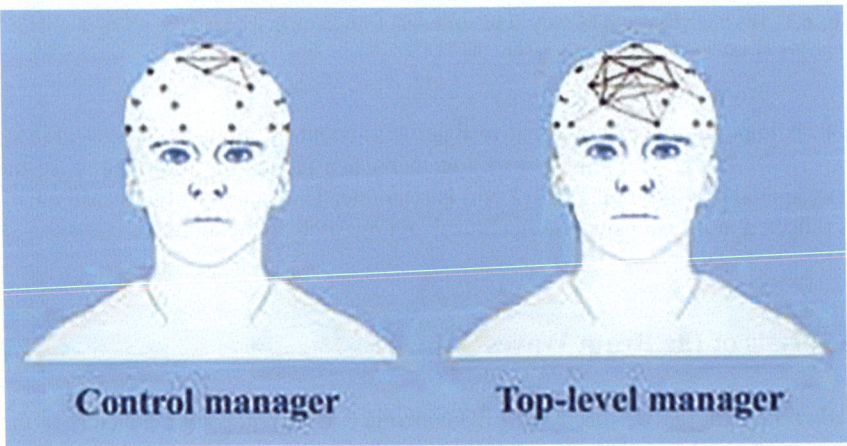

Fig. 6.3 Coherence maps of a control manager and top-level manager (The figure shows the brain wave coherence between various areas of the frontal cortex in a typical low-level manager compared to a typical top-level manager in our research. When there is a line between two points this means that the brain waves at those points are at least 70% in coherence with each other. The darker the line, the stronger the coherence)

athletes was different from that of their controls. The high performers responded in a more efficient way in preparation for both reaction tests.

Brain-To-Brain Synchrony

Hyperscanning. We have discussed brain coherence within individuals. With the ongoing development of EEG recording equipment and signal analysis software, researchers have recently been able to look at brain coherence between individuals. That's right—the coherence of the EEG signals from a point on the scalp of one individual with the signals from the same point on another person. This is called *hyperscanning* and can be used to probe the quality of interactions between people.

In the first study we will cite, the researchers wrote: "We used EEG to simultaneously record brain activity from groups of four students and a teacher in a simulated classroom setting to investigate whether brain-to-brain synchrony, both between students and between the students and the teacher, can predict learning outcomes. We found that brain-to-brain synchrony in the alpha band (8–12 cycles per second or Hz) predicted students' delayed memory retention."[5]

A second study found that hyperscanning of pairs of pilots in a simulated flying condition matched the level of cooperation between the pilots in different phases of the flight—greater cooperation during take-off and landing was associated with high brain-to-brain synchrony in frontal and parietal brain areas.[6]

A third study reported that when one person watches a movie alone on one day, and another person watches the same movie alone on another day, there is a significant brain-to-brain synchrony between them during the same parts of the film. This suggests that brain-to-brain synchrony simply reflects similar cognitive processes used to interpret a similar external stimulus.[7]

Brain-to-brain synchrony is a phenomenon that can be explained by classical models, i.e., by information that is transmitted through our senses (especially eyes and hearing) and behavior. Hyperscanning will therefore play a role in the behavior of notably teams, where there is extensive direct interaction between people. And to a lesser extent in organizations, where the direct interaction between members may overall be less—especially for large and/or multinational organizations (see Chapter 10).

Field effect of consciousness. In Chapter 11 we explore the possibility that people—even at a large distance from each other—may be affected by the complementary field effect of consciousness. A field has *non-local* properties that influence events across space. Well-known examples in the physical world are the gravitational and electromagnetic fields. Due to the non-local properties of the electromagnetic

---

[5] Davidesco et al. (2023).

[6] Toppi et al. (2016).

[7] Hamilton (2021).

field, you can use your cell phone to talk to your friend on the other side of the globe as if she or he is next door to you.

In Chapter 11 we provide evidence that consciousness is also an underlying field. This quantum mechanical influence will broaden the understanding of how people interact in the larger society and even in the whole world.

To provide a complete picture, it should be noted that the field effect of consciousness seems also to play a part in the interaction between people who are close to each other, i.e., as a complementary influence to hyperscanning. A study used a random-assignment, double-blind design to probe effects of nine students practicing the Transcendental Meditation technique on the subjective experiences and physiological patterns of another meditating student sitting in the adjacent room who was unaware of the presence of the larger group. When the group was meditating, the individual (receiver) reported more settled meditation experiences, and exhibited higher alpha EEG power, a correlate of deep meditation experiences.[8]

* * *

That was a lot of neural science in a few pages. We hope this chapter has given you a little better understanding of what it means to have an integrated brain and how that's measured. Now, of course, the obvious question is how you can develop a more integrated brain. That will be the topic of the next two chapters.

References

Davidesco, I., Laurent, E., Valk, H., West, T., Milne, C., Poeppel, D., & Dikker, S. (2023). The temporal dynamics of brain-to-brain synchrony between students and teachers predict learning outcomes. *Psychological Science, 34*(5), 633–643.

Hamilton, A. F. C. (2021, February 3). Hyperscanning: Beyond the hype. *Neuron, 109*(3), 404–407. Epub 2020 Nov 30. PMID: 33259804.

Holden, C. (1979, June 8). Paul MacLean and the triune brain. *Science, 204*(4397), 1066–1068.

Kleinschnitz, K., & Travis, F. (2024). Testing the Field Nature of Consciousness: A Pilot Test | Kleinschnitz | *International Journal of Psychological Studies* | CCSE (ccsenet.org). https://doi.org/10.5539/ijps.v16n2p63. Retrieved July 25, 2024.

Storm, J. F. (2014, April 6). På sporet av bevisstheten (On the track of consciousness). *Aftenposten*, pp. 12–13.

Toppi, J., Borghini, G., Petti, M., He, E. J., De Giusti, V., He, B., Astolfi, L., & Babiloni, F. (2016). Investigating cooperative behavior in ecological settings: An EEG hyperscanning study. *PLoS One*. https://doi.org/10.1371/journal.pone.0154236. Retrieved October 12, 2024.

Travis, F. (2012). Your brain is a river, not a rock. Fairfield, Iowa, USA. www.amazon.com.

---

[8] Kleinschnitz & Travis (2024).

Chapter 7
How to Develop Brain Integration

Abstract There are two complementary processes to refine the brain. First, in Chapter 1 we described how the expression of genes guides natural brain maturation up to the age of 25. Second, the present chapter examines how ongoing experiences, through neuroplasticity, open up the possibility of lifelong brain refinement through appropriate lifestyle choices. In particular, we'll consider getting enough sleep, physical exercise, playing and listening to music, and transcendence through meditation practice.

It seems clear from the three studies we describe in this book that integrated brain functioning is associated with high performance. But what about cause and effect? Are some people simply born with a more integrated brain and therefore spontaneously able to be world-class performers? Or do world-class performers, by virtue of their diligent practice and performance, develop an integrated brain, and this greater integration then allows them to excel? In other words, is it nature or nurture?

We think that both play a role. We are born with strengths and preferences; our life experiences shape our innate abilities into who we are at any moment. Thus, our present level of mind-brain development depends on the interaction of both:

$$\text{Mind} - \text{brain development} = \text{Nature} + \text{Nurture}$$

in which:

- *Nature* consists of our genetic endowment, including each individual's physical and mental traits, tendencies, and talents; and the natural tendency to grow towards higher states of consciousness, which we all share. This theme was introduced in Chapter 1.
- *Nurture* consists of the sum of our experiences in life. This includes family experiences; social experiences in school and with friends; and the choices we make for different lifestyles, different vocations, and different paths in life. Nurture even extends out to the society and time we are born into.

© The Author(s), under exclusive license to Springer Nature Switzerland AG 2025
H. S. Harung and F. Travis, *World-Class Brain*,
https://doi.org/10.1007/978-3-031-86667-8_7

Nurture is the topic of this chapter. To illustrate the effect of the social context where children and youth grow up, a recent study[1] found that their neighborhood influences their possibilities later in life, but parents and family are more important because they can buffer the effects of environmental stress.

We are not passive "victims" who are controlled by our upbringing or genetic endowment. Rather, our ongoing life experiences strengthen specific brain circuits, shape our stress response, and even shape expression of our genetic code. Our diet, our ongoing experience, and the level of stress or harmony in life add tags to our DNA—tags that influence genetic expression, leading to reduced immune functioning and greater illness, or to good health, happiness, and a long life. These tags are part of *epigenetics*, which literally means "above the gene." Lifestyle is very important here.

In this chapter we introduce four ways to develop mind-brain integration through lifestyle choices. In Chapter 8 we discuss in more detail the power of the most important of these ways—transcending—to facilitate positive genetic expression throughout life. This is good news since it gives us the possibility to take part in programming our epigenetics. Thus, we are more in control of our mind-brain development and our life.

Lifelong Development

Let's go deeper into the possibility of lifelong development. We discussed in Chapter 1 how natural, innate processes shape brain circuits for the first 25 years of life. In addition, throughout childhood, experiences amplify or dampen natural development. Since brain development normally stops in the early twenties, psychological development also tends to remain stable after that age.[2]

Fred[3] has written a book entitled *Your Brain Is a River, Not a Rock*. This book paints the picture of the brain as a self-adapting organ, which constantly changes to support more effective behavior. This constant change is called *neuroplasticity*. Think of an analogy with your muscles. If you do a lot of pushups, your arm and chest muscles will grow stronger. If you don't exercise, your muscles will weaken. The muscle groups you use and how much you use them determines the strength and size of your muscles. Similarly, brain circuits build up the more you use them.

---

[1] Brattbakk & Andersen (2017).

[2] Cohn (1998), Harung & Travis (2016).

[3] Travis (2012).

Neuroplasticity—The Brain Changes with Every Experience

Neuroplasticity is a hot area of research today. There are many examples of how the ability of the brain to adapt to new circumstances has advantages for performance. A four-year study[4] examined brain connections in London taxi drivers. To become licensed as a taxi driver in this huge city you have to build up extensive knowledge about the quickest route from one place to another, essentially outperforming the GPS. The study involved three groups of men:

1. Forty-one who started training for their license and who later passed the test.
2. Thirty-eight who started training to become a licensed taxi driver, but who later dropped out or were not able to pass the test.
3. Thirty-one *non*-taxi-drivers of similar ages who served as controls.

The research investigated the size of the *hippocampus*, the part of our brain that is engaged in memory, including spatial navigation. At pretest, brain scans using fMRI found no differences between the three groups. But at post-test the rear part of the hippocampus had grown to become significantly larger in the taxi drivers who had become licensed, while there was no change for the other two groups. The experienced taxi drivers also had larger hippocampal volumes than experienced London bus drivers who drove the same route each day.

Similarly, an fMRI study[5] in China has shown that top athletes have more brain matter in areas associated with learning and processing movement.

Neuroplasticity takes place throughout life. It is part of the mechanism that facilitates mind-brain development in adults.

In conclusion, due to neuroplasticity our brain changes and develops depending on how we use it. This suggests that the world-class performers we studied had integrated brains because of both nature—their genetic endowment—and their ongoing life experience. And in turn, having an integrated brain facilitated their performance, just as developing better mind–body coordination facilitates performance in all sports and in playing all types of music.

Four Complementary Ways to Develop Brain Integration Throughout Life

The choices we make lead to specific experiences, which strengthen specific brain circuits. Research suggests four *complementary* experiences that contribute to higher brain integration throughout life: Get a good night's sleep, add exercise to your daily routine, take time for music and the visual arts, and practice a meditation technique that leads to transcending. Of course, a healthy diet and a rich social network are also good for the brain, but this is outside the scope of this book.

---

[4] Woollett & Maguire (2011).

[5] Wei et al. (2011).

1. ***Value of a good night's sleep.*** Why do we sleep? Why do we spend 1/3 of our life with our eyes closed and not being productive? Actually, we are being productive. Sleep is removing the effects of being awake. Recent research[6] published in *Science* reports that we create 7 g of "dirt" in the brain during the day. This dirt includes degraded neurotransmitters and enzymes, proteins that are not completely metabolized. During sleep, structural components of the brain constrict, resulting in a 60% increase in the space around each cell. This increases the movement of cerebrospinal fluid around the cell, removing the dirt. Sleep gives the brain a bath.

   Sleep deprivation reduces learning, impairs cognitive functioning,[7] and is tied to the onset of dementia.[8] In addition, as you get more tired throughout the day, the first part of your brain to slow down is the frontal cortex. The CEO goes offline. You become more emotional and less able to see the big picture. Thus, sleep is critical for a healthy mind and body and a high level of performance.

   A recent study of Norwegian adolescents reports that sleep is recognized as a crucial factor for children's and adolescents' health and wellbeing. Sleep problems thus influence physical, psychic, social, and emotional development. Unfortunately, inadequate sleep is frequently reported in numerous countries. The Norwegian research found: "This cross-sectional study demonstrated that almost three out of four Norwegian adolescents did not meet the sleep recommendations ... Screen time negatively affected their ability to get enough sleep. Findings revealed a positive association between adhering to the 8-h of sleep recommendation and satisfaction with life."[9]

2. ***Adequate exercise.*** The more physically fit you are, the better you can withstand stress. Higher fitness is tied to faster brain processing of information. The more times a student can run around a track is positively and significantly correlated with higher performance on standardized academic tests such as the SAT or GRE.[10]

   Why is this the case? When you exercise four things happen. First, cardio-vascular functioning improves. You can do more work without getting tired and feeling stressed. Second, when you exercise, your heart beats faster, bringing more oxygen to your body. At the same time, you're bringing more oxygen to your brain. You know how you feel after even a short run—everything is brighter and fuller. Third, when you exercise you produce more new brain cells in the hippocampus. Fourth, exercising leads to increased concentration of a brain-derived neural growth substance that supports neuroplasticity. So, exercising

---

[6] Xie et al. (2013).

[7] Stickgold (2006).

[8] Montagna et al. (2003).

[9] Grasaas et al. (2024).

[10] Castelli et al. (2007).

enriches the brain with oxygen, primes the memory centers of the brain, facilitates neural changes to enhance memory, and opens up the possibility of brain refinement.

Let us consider research illustrating the benefits of physical exercise. First, findings published in the journal *Memory*, show that there is a consistent association between sports and better working memory performance, while a sedentary lifestyle appears to be associated with poorer working memory. Furthermore, a physically active lifestyle can partly mitigate the negative effects of aging.[11]

Second,[12] sufficient exercise throughout life is also important for good physical and mental health and well-being, which provides the basis for our performance. A recent review of 57 articles found that high-level athletes live on average 5 years longer than the general population.[13]

3. ***Enjoying music and engaging in the arts.*** The arts are important. Math and language develop localized brain circuits—there is one right answer. In contrast, musical training facilitates more holistic brain development: It increases connections between the left and right hemispheres, since you need to focus on the specific notes and how to play them at the same time that you maintain attention on the longer melody line.

Playing an instrument is reported[14] to lead to extensive changes in brain functioning. It supports the ability to distinguish a tone from background noise, and develops brain areas relevant to remembering a score, timing issues, and coordination with other musicians. In addition, musical training is reported to strengthen connections between auditory and motor regions while activating brain areas that put everything together.

While most research has investigated specific effects of music practice, some studies have also reported differences between professional and amateur musicians in overall brain functioning.[15] Frontal brain areas—involved in planning, guiding mental and behavioral sequences, and controlling responses—are more extensively activated during performance in professional musicians compared to non-musicians. Research using fMRI revealed reduced brain activation during motor tasks in piano players compared to control subjects. This was explained in terms of more efficient brain wiring leading to lower neural activation.

Although playing music probably gives the largest benefits, there are also benefits from listening to music. A study[16] found that brain connectivity was highest when listening to *preferred* music.

---

[11] Wu et al. (2024).

[12] Penedo & Dahn (2005), Haskell et al. (2007).

[13] Gervais (2024).

[14] Hyde et al. (2009a, 2009b).

[15] Zuk et al. (2014).

[16] Wilkins et al. (2014).

Research[17] at the University of Arts in London concluded that secondary education students who learn about art and culture achieve better grades in all disciplines.

4. *Meditation Practices.* There is a wide range of meditation techniques available today that differ in the amount of control used during the practice. Different meditation techniques lead to distinctly different brain wave patterns and subjective experiences:

- *Focused attention* meditations require the most effort, e.g., Zen meditation. Meditations in this category may focus on one part of the body or focus on the breath or a compassionate mood. Whenever you focus attention, faster gamma brain waves (20–50 Hz) dominate in the brain (see Table 6.2).
- *Open monitoring* meditations require less control than those in the first category. During open monitoring practices, such as mindfulness meditation, you dispassionately observe internal processes, such the breath, bodily states, thoughts, or feelings that may arise. This results in frontal theta brain waves (5–8 Hz) and alpha2 brain waves (10–12 Hz) towards the upper back (parietal lobe) of the brain, indicating that one is following inner mental processes (see Table 6.2).
- *Automatic self-transcending.* The Transcendental Meditation® (TM®) technique is a simple mental technique that is practiced for 20 min morning and evening and that involves automatic self-transcending. During this technique the mind settles down to deeper and deeper levels of consciousness. This settling down is facilitated by the *effortless* thinking of a mantra, a sound without meaning. When we go deep in this meditation, we transcend, which means to go beyond. Transcendence is the most fundamental and expanded mental level.

In this book we will focus on Transcendental Meditation which is structured for transcending. The TM technique is characterized by heightened alpha1 (8–10 Hz) brain waves in the front of the brain, indicating that the attention is awake and inner-directed. The word "automatic" is important for this meditation. Any focusing or control of the mind leads to localized brain activity and does not allow the mind to settle down to inner silence.

Different effects on the brain of different meditations. Let us elaborate on the different effects on the brain of different meditations:

- First, consider an experience during mindfulness meditation: "... discontinuation in awareness similar to the loss of consciousness, which are reported to be experienced by very experienced meditators and are proposed to be evidence of mastery of mindfulness meditation ... Spectral analyses of the EEG data surrounding cessations showed that these events were marked by a large-scale alpha-power decrease ...."[18] In sharp contrast, we have in this book seen that the deepest and

---

[17] Tessem (2011).
[18] Chowdhury et al. (2023).

most rewarding experiences of the TM technique — which are marked by continuation of awareness but no content — are characterized by maximum alertness and high alpha 1 power.

- Second, a recent paper reported that during Transcendental Meditation practice default mode network (DMN) activity remains high.[19] The default mode network is a name for brain areas in the front (central medial prefrontal cortex) and back (precuneus) where the activity is high when the attention is freely moving without control. In contrast, activity in the default mode network goes down during goal-directed thinking. Therefore, default mode network activity is reduced during meditation practices in the first two categories and remains high in TM.

- To summarize, meditations in the focused attention and open monitoring categories require active mental processing—active thinking. In contrast, meditations in the automatic self-transcending category, such as Transcendental Meditation, start with normal thinking but end up with a substantial reduction in mental activity or transcendence—a state in which one is aware but without an object of thought.

Different overall effects of different meditations. Extensive research shows that regular and long-term practice of the Transcendental Meditation technique leads to large cumulative benefits. The long-term studies have lasted for up to 20 years. The conclusion is that the more regular you are and the longer you meditate, the larger are the positive effects.

Several large research reviews have now been done that compare the effects of various mental techniques. A number of these meta-analyses have found that the TM technique has significantly greater benefits than the others. For example, Dr. Kenneth R. Eppley at Stanford University and his team considered 146 studies and found that Transcendental Meditation was about twice as effective as the other methods in reducing anxiety.[20] And Professor Peter Sedlmeier at the Technische Universität Chemnitz in Germany and his co-workers examined 21 studies and found that the TM technique was about three times more effective in reducing negative emotions compared to mindfulness and about twice as effective compared to other meditations.[21]

Also, several recent studies have suggested that mindfulness meditation may be associated with some serious negative side-effects. The unwanted effects include increased anxiety, emotional numbness, and sleep disturbances. The types of mindfulness techniques producing these effects were focused attention on breathing, body scan, and open monitoring, also called "observing awareness." In other words, this research seemed to include both focused attention and open monitoring, as described above.[22]

---

[19] Travis and Parim (2017).

[20] Eppley et al. (1989).

[21] Sedlmeier et al. (2012).

[22] Robson (2021), Schlosser et al. (2019), Britton (2019), Cebolla et al. (2017), Britton et al. (2010).

More about research on Transcendental Meditation. Why is TM more beneficial than the other categories of meditation techniques? A new study[23] confirms that the practice of the TM technique leads to a distinctive state of rest and wakefulness—called *restful alertness*—that is not found in other meditations. Functional magnetic resonance imagining (fMRI) patterns of 16 subjects during their practice of Transcendental Meditation found that, like meditations that involve focused attention or open monitoring, there was increased blood flow activity in the areas of the prefrontal cortex related to attention—indicating alertness. However, unlike other meditations, during Transcendental Meditation there was also decreased activity in the areas related to arousal—indicating deep rest.

Let us illustrate the extensive long-term benefits of TM by summarizing two research projects:

1. A randomized study of US elderly heart patients involved the American Heart Association and was funded with USD 3.8 million by the National Institutes of Health (NIH). This controlled trial lasted up to 10 years (mean of 5.4 years) and found that those who on average practiced TM 8.5 times per week (61% regular), had a 48% reduction in the risk of heart attacks, strokes, and death compared with Health Education (learning about nutrition and exercise) controls. Those who on average practiced TM 11.6 times per week (83% regular) had 66% fewer clinical events than controls.[24]

2. A 10-year investigation of ego or self-development of students at Maharishi International University in the US concluded that the number of TM-meditating subjects who scored on the mature self-actualizing stage increased from 9% at pre-test (these subjects had already been meditating for several years) to 38% at post-test. These students also practiced the advanced TM-Sidhi® program that some people enjoy as an addition to Transcendental Meditation. In comparison, 1% of the control students at three other universities were found to be functioning from this level at both pre-test and post-test. About 1% reaching self-actualization is the norm today.[25]

Since different procedures have different intentions and result in different brain patterns, the practical benefits in daily life differ from technique to technique, as substantiated by extensive research.[26] It falls outside the scope of this short book to consider in depth the different types of meditation. Instead, we will, as said, focus on Transcendental Meditation for the following reasons:

- The TM technique develops all three aspects of the Brain Integration Scale.
- It also develops the three other dimensions of the *Unified Theory of Performance* (please refer to the Afterword).

---

[23] Mahone et al. (2018).

[24] Schneider et al. (2012).

[25] Chandler et al. (2005).

[26] Orme-Johnson & Walton (1998), Travis & Shear (2010), Harung & Travis (2016).

- In fact, this technique has a wide range of substantial benefits, including improvements in health, creativity, intelligence, memory, performance in general, and social trends (see Chapter 11).
- Research has shown that the longer you practice TM and the more regular you are in your practice, the larger are the benefits.
- Extensive research has shown that the TM technique has a larger and wider range of benefits than other researched mental practices, some of which may, in fact, even cause problems with long and/or regular practice, as just seen.
- As far as we know, benefits for brain integration and society (See Chapter 11) have not been studied for other meditations.
- The technique is accessible—it is easy, effortless, and enjoyable.
- The TM technique is taught globally in a standardized way by well-trained teachers.

Transcending is Key to Develop Brain Integration

Recall our finding that high performers have high brain integration. Research on the Transcendental Meditation technique shows that transcending leads to higher levels of brain integration.[27]

Figure 7.1 presents brain integration for four groups of subjects:

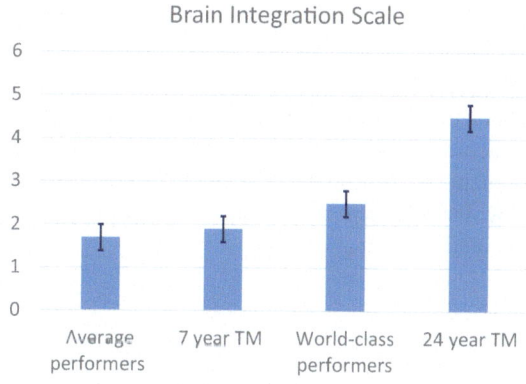

Fig. 7.1 Levels of brain integration in different groups (This figure shows the Brain Integration Scale scores of (1) Average performers in our database, including the controls of our three world-class studies, (2) Individuals with short-term TM practice (7 years), (3) The world-class athletes, managers, and musicians who we studied, and (4) Individuals with long-term TM practice (24 years), who were also practicing the advanced TM-Sidhi program during the last part of the 24 years. All persons included here were at least 25 years of age)

---

[27] Travis et al. (2009).

1. Average performers in our database, including the controls of our three world-class performance studies.
2. Individuals with short-term TM practice (7 years).
3. The world-class athletes, managers, and musicians who we studied.
4. Individuals with long-term TM practice (24 years).

As seen, long-term practice of Transcendental Meditation is associated with brain integration far beyond that of the top performers in our three studies.

Notice in the figure that the top-level performers have Brain Integration Scale scores a little higher than the short-term TM group, but only about half that of the long-term TM group. Obviously, many factors contribute to high levels of brain integration in the peak performers, as seen above. However, the data suggest that adding repeated transcending to one's daily routine could enhance brain integration, leading to enhanced performance. In Chapters 8 and 10 we introduce research that has already been done on the benefits of TM for performance. More research is needed here.

We are in this book quoting several *spontaneous* peak experiences enjoyed by the world-class performers, often in relation to optimal performance. Such moments, which in many cases involve transcendence, are completely natural. Obviously, the peak performers (and the controls) would like to have many more such delightful experiences, but the challenge is that peaks can't normally be consciously triggered. Therefore, the next chapter will further explore Transcendental Meditation, a simple technique for systematically facilitating transcendence.

* * *

In this chapter we have considered the importance of lifestyle in gene expression. We have introduced neuroplasticity as a mechanism whereby lifelong brain refinement can be achieved. We have also seen that transcending is the key to mind-brain development. We devote the next chapter to understanding further what transcending is, how Transcendental Meditation works, and its many benefits for enhancing happiness and performance.

References

Brattbakk, I., & Andersen, B. (2017). Oppvekststedets betydning for barn og unge — nabolaget som ressurs og utfordring (The significance of the place where children and youth grow up — neighborhood as a resource and challenge). *AFI Rapport* 2.

Britton, W. B., Hayens, P. L., Fridel, K. W., & Booztin, R. R. (2010). Polysomnographic and subjective profiles of sleep continuity before and after mindfulness-based cognitive therapy in partially remitted depression. *Psychosomatic Medicine, 72*(6), 539–548.

Britton. W. B. (2019, August). Can mindfulness be too much of a good thing? The value of a middle way. *Current Opinion in Psychology, 28*, 159–165.

Castelli, D. M., Hillman, C. H., Buck, S. M., & Erwin, H. E. (2007). Physical fitness and academic achievement in third- and fifth-grade students. *Journal of Sport Exercise Psychology, 29*(2), 239–52.

Cebolla, C., Demarzo, M., Martins P., et al. (2017). https://www.researchgate.net/publication/319 495500_Unwanted_effects_Is_there_a_negative_side_of_meditation_A_multicentre_survey# fullTextFileContent. Retrieved October 12, 2024.

Chandler, H., Alexander, C., Heaton, D., & Grant, J. (2005). Transcendental Meditation and post-conventional self-development: A 10-year longitudinal study. *Journal of Social Behavior and Personality, 17*(1), 93–122.

Chowdhury, A., et al. (2023). *Neuropsychologia.* Investigation of advanced mindfulness meditation "cessation" experiences using EEG spectral analysis in an intensively sampled case study (vu.nl). https://doi.org/10.1016/j.neuropsychologia.2023.108694. Retrieved July 25, 2024.

Cohn, L. D. (1998). Age trends in personality development: A quantitative review. In P. M. Westenberg, A. Blasi, & L. D. Cohn (Eds.), *Personality development: Theoretical, empirical and clinical investigations of Loevinger's conception of ego development* (pp. 133–143). Lawrence Erlbaum Associates.

Eppley, K. R., Abrams, A. I., & Shear, J. (1989, November). Differential effects of relaxation techniques on trait anxiety: A meta-analysis. *Journal of Clinical Psychology*.https://doi.org/10. 1002/1097-4679(198911)45:6<957::AID-JCLP2270450622>3.0.CO;2-Q. Retrieved October 12, 2024.

Gervais, J.-B. (2024). Do top athletes live longer and better lives? https://www.medscape.com/vie warticle/do-top-athletes-live-better-and-longer-lives-2024a1000cou?form=fpf. Retrieved July 25, 2024.

Grasaas, E., Ostojic, S., & Jahre, H. (2024). Adherence to sleep recommendations is associated with higher satisfaction with life among Norwegian adolescents. *BMC Public Health.* https://doi.org/10.1186/s12889-024-18725-1. Retrieved September 6, 2024.

Harung, H. S., & Travis, F. (2016). *Excellence through mind-brain development: The secrets of world-class performers.* Routledge.

Haskell, W. L., et al. (2007). Physical activity and public health: Updated recommendation for adults from the American College of Sports Medicine and the American Heart Association. *Circulation, 116*(9), 1081–1093.

Hyde, K. L., Lerch, J., Norton, A., Forgeard, M., Winner, E., & Evans, A. C. (2009). Musical training shapes structural brain development. *Journal of Neuroscience, 29*(10), 3019–3025.

Hyde, K. L., Lerch, L., Norton, A., Forgeard, M., Winner, E., Evans, A. C., & Schlaug, G. (2009). The effects of musical training on structural brain development: A longitudinal study. The neurosciences and music III: Disorders and plasticity. *Annals of the New York Academy of Sciences, 1169*, 182–186.

Mahone, M. C., Travis, F., Gevirtz, R., & Hubbard, D. (2018). FMRI during transcendental meditation practice. *Brain and Cognition, 123*, 30–33.

Montagna, P., Gambetti, P., Cortelli, P., & Lugaresi, E. (2003). Familial and sporadic fatal insomnia. *Lancet Neuro, 2*, 167–176.

Orme-Johnson, D. W., & Walton, K. G. (1998). All approaches to preventing and reversing the effects of stress are not the same. *American Journal of Health Promotion, 12*(5), 297–299.

Penedo, F. J., & Dahn, J. R. (2005). Exercise and well-being: A review of mental and physical health benefits associated with physical activity. *Current Opinion in Psychiatry, 18*(2), 189–193. https://doi.org/10.1097/00001504-200503000-00013

Robson, D. (2021). How too much mindfulness can spike anxiety. *BBC Worklife.* https://www.bbc.com/worklife/article/20210202-how-mindfulness-can-blunt-your-feelings-and-spike-anxiety. Retrieved September 19, 2024.

Schlosser, M., Sparby, T., Vörös, S., et al. (2019). Unpleasant meditation-related experiences in regular meditators: Prevalence, predictors, and conceptual considerations. *PLoS ONE*, Pud Med, May 9.

Schneider, R. H., Grim, C. E., Rainforth, M. A., et al. (2012). Stress reduction in the secondary prevention of cardiovascular disease: Randomized controlled trial of Transcendental Meditation and health education in Blacks. *Circulation: Cardiovascular Quality Outcomes, 5*(6), 750–758.

Sedlmeier, P., Eberth, J., Schwarz, M., Zimmermann, D., Haarig, F., Jaeger, S., & Kunze, S. (2012). The psychological effects of meditation: A meta-analysis. *Psychological Bulletin, 138,* 1139–1171. https://doi.org/10.1037/a0028168

Stickgold, R. (2006, November 30). Neuroscience: A memory boost while you sleep. *Nature, 444*(7119), 559–560. PubMed PMID: 17086196.

Tessem, L. B. (2011, March). Kunst gir bedre karakterer (Art gives better grades). *Aftenposten, 14,* 5.

Travis, F., & Shear, J. (2010). Focused attention, open monitoring and automatic self-transcending: Categories to organize meditations from Vedic, Buddhist and Chinese traditions. *Consciousness and Cognition, 19,* 1110–1119.

Travis, F. (2012). *Your brain is a river, not a rock.* Fairfield. www.amazon.com.

Travis, F., & Parim, N. (2017). Default mode network activation and transcendental meditation practice: Focused attention or automatic self-transcending? *Brain and Cognition, 111,* 86–94.

Travis, F., Haaga, D. H., Hagelin, J., Tanner, M., Nidich, S., Gaylord-King, C., Grosswald, S., Rainforth, M., & Schneider, R. (2009). Effects of Transcendental Meditation practice on brain functioning and stress reactivity in college students. *International Journal of Psychophysiology, 71,* 170–176.

Wei, G., Zhang, Y., Jiang, T., & Luo, J. (2011). Increased cortical thickness in sports experts: A comparison of diving players with the controls. *Plos One.* https://doi.org/10.1371/journal.pone.0017112. Retrieved July 25, 2024.

Wilkins, R. W., Hodges, D. A., Laurienti, P. J., Steen, M., & Burdette, J. H. (2014, August 4). Network science and the effects of music preference on functional brain connectivity: From Beethoven to Eminem. *Scientific Reports.*

Woollett, K., & Maguire, E. A. (2011). Acquiring "the knowledge" of London's layout drives structural brain changes. *Current Biology, 21,* 2109–2114.

Wu, C., Zhang, C., Li, X., Ye, C., & Astikainen, P. (2024). Comparison of working memory performance in athletes and non-athletes: A meta-analysis of behavioural studies. *Memory, 1–19,* 2024.

Xie, L., Kang, H., Xu, Q., Chen, M. J., Liao, Y., Thiyagarajan, M., O'Donnell, J., Christensen, D. J., Nicholson, C., Iliff, J. J., Takano, T., Deane, R., & Nedergaard, M. (2013). Sleep drives metabolite clearance from the adult brain. *Science.* https://doi.org/10.1126/science.1241224. Retrieved July 25, 2024.

Zuk, J., Benjamin, C., Kenyon, A., & Gaab, N. (2014). Behavioral and neural correlates of executive functioning in musicians and non-musicians. *Plos One.* https://doi.org/10.1371/journal.pone.0099868. Retrieved July 25, 2024.

Chapter 8
How Transcendental Meditation Develops Brain Integration

Abstract This chapter considers in more depth the Transcendental Meditation technique. Research shows that this effortless technique enhances all three components of the Brain Integration Scale. We also present personal accounts of people enjoying the practice of this technique, and evidence of the benefits from transcendence within a wide range of areas, including intuition, creativity, health, and performance.

The previous chapter gave an overview of different approaches to brain integration. We established that systematic transcending during the Transcendental Meditation technique showed the most promise, and therefore in this chapter we'll go more deeply into the wide range of benefits of this simple technique.

The Transcendental Meditation technique enables us to systematically reduce mental activity, leading us towards transcending thought and to experience the inner silence at the source of thought.[1] Experiencing deep inner silence gives us an inner anchor to cope with the accelerating dynamics of life.

The experience of transcending leads also to higher brain integration. The brain underlies thinking and behavior. Brain integration will therefore result in favorable changes in emotions, thinking, and behavior.

What is Transcendental Meditation?

How does the Transcendental Meditation technique work? It's a simple technique practiced for 20 min twice a day sitting comfortably with the eyes closed. One learns from a certified teacher, with the course taking about 1–2 h a day over four days. Learning the technique itself just takes minutes—a couple of simple steps and you're meditating. The rest of the time is taken up explaining how it works, what the benefits are, and the tradition the technique comes from, as well as answering questions. After the initial instruction, there is a follow-up program to ensure effortless, enjoyable,

---

[1] Maharishi ([1963] 2001).

© The Author(s), under exclusive license to Springer Nature Switzerland AG 2025
H. S. Harung and F. Travis, *World-Class Brain*,
https://doi.org/10.1007/978-3-031-86667-8_8

and thus effective practice. The internationally standardized steps enable the new meditator to be well established in the practice after only a few days.

The hallmark of Transcendental Meditation is its *effortlessness*. One doesn't try to focus or concentrate. Instead, one learns how to use the natural tendency of the mind to take attention from active thinking to the silence at the source of thought.[2] As your mind settles down, the level of functioning of your sympathetic nervous system—the fight-or-flight system—is reset to a more relaxed functioning.[3] For example, while you meditate, there are changes to your blood chemistry, including a reduction in hormones such as cortisol and lactate that are associated with stress. In addition, a measure of galvanic skin response indicates that your perspiration decreases, a sign of greater relaxation. Blood flow to the frontal cortex of the brain increases, indicating enhanced wakefulness.

Brain Changes During Transcendental Meditation Practice

And your brain waves change. Right from the very early days of your practice, your brain shows increased frontal alpha1 coherence while you're meditating. This brain signature signals that the mind is at its ground state—silent and awake.

In fact, during the practice high levels of alpha1 coherence are already seen after just a few months of TM practice. Thereafter, what changes with regular practice is that the inner experience and the brain signature of inner wakefulness become integrated with daily activity. As one meditates month after month, year after year, this alpha1 coherence is increasingly present *outside* of meditation, providing an enhanced basis for processing experience and for performance.

This is illustrated by Fig. 8.1. The upper part shows the alpha1 coherence during the TM technique of a person who had been meditating four months (left) compared to a person who had been meditating for eight years (right). The coherence is very similar. This is because TM practice is effortless, using the natural tendency of the mind to transcend. Consequently, individuals quickly master transcending during Transcendental Meditation practice. Additional practice does not make a natural process go any better, as illustrated by the figure.

The lower part of this figure presents a comparison of the same two people with their eyes open during a challenging computer task. The person on the right, who has been meditating for eight years, shows the same brain coherence as during TM, even with his eyes open and engaged in a task. In contrast, the brain of the person meditating for only four months has much less alpha1 coherence during activity.

---

[2] Travis & Parim (2017).
[3] Dillbeck & Orme-Johnson (1987).

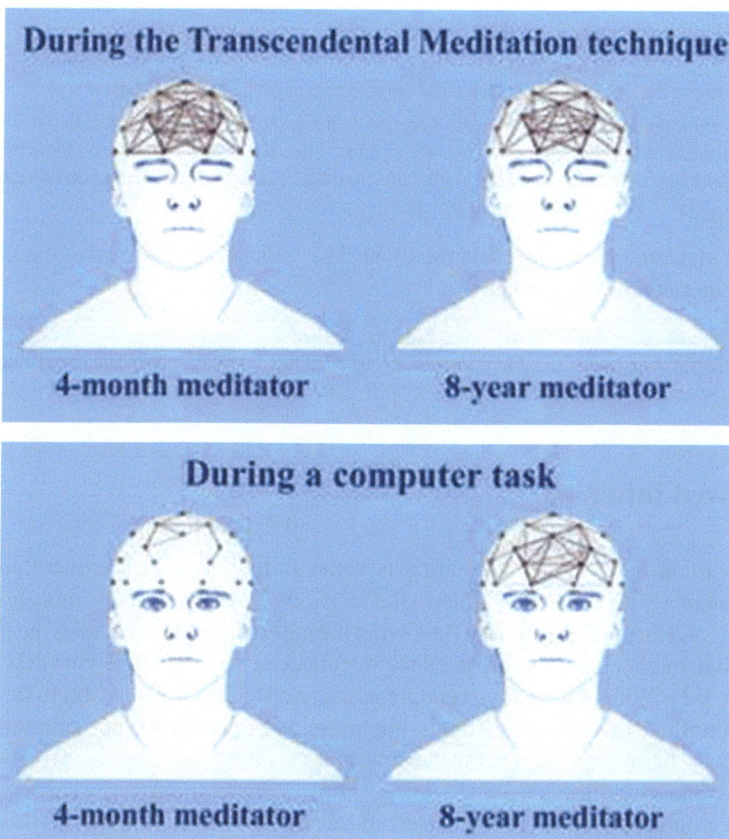

Fig. 8.1 EEG coherence for 4-month and 8-year meditators (This figure shows that during the practice of Transcendental Meditation [upper part] there is little difference between a four-month and an eight-year meditator, while outside meditation the difference is much larger between these two [lower part])

Personal Accounts of Benefits from Transcendence

Let's take a look at some of the benefits of the experience of transcendence. David Lynch, the late director and writer behind the TV series *Twin Peaks* and movies including *Mulholland Drive*, was a daily practitioner of Transcendental Meditation. According to an article in *Los Angeles Times*,[4] he said, "Transcendental Meditation is the secret to success." David did not miss a day of meditation in over 50 years:

> … TM is the secret to … well, everything … So many illnesses are called stress-related illness and stress can kill you. … Stress can shut down so much in a human being. If you want to get rid of it, you transcend every day. … There is a line, 'know thyself'… It's a beautiful,

[4] Dawson (2016).

beautiful thing to experience that. ... True happiness is not 'out there;' true happiness lies within.

Replying to the question "How does TM enhance creativity?" David replies:

You want more ideas, you want more energy to do the work and more happiness in the doing — where are all of these things? They are within... I think ideas are out there and you catch them like how you catch fish. The more consciousness you have, the deeper you can catch those ideas."

Sir Paul McCartney[5] recently said this about TM, which he and the rest of the Beatles learned more than 55 years ago:

In moments of madness, [TM] meditation has helped me find moments of serenity. ... I think meditation offers a moment in your day to be at peace with yourself and therefore the universe.

Improved Intuition

One common benefit of transcending is better intuition. Basically, there are two complementary ways that our brains make decisions.[6] First is the quick, more holistic, intuitive, and instinctive response (involving the inner brain), and second is the longer, sequential, intellectual response in which we reflect on the issue (involving the cortex. See Fig. 6.1). With regular transcending and associated higher mind-brain development, intuition becomes increasingly important and reliable. At the same time, the two approaches increasingly act in synergy, and the intellectual approach can be used to check one's intuition.

This double approach is illustrated in an article[7] about Magnus Carlsen, the Norwegian chess player who, as of 2024, is a five-time World Chess Champion, the reigning five-time World Rapid Chess Champion, the reigning seven-time World Blitz Chess Champion, and the reigning Chess World Cup Champion, with the highest chess rating in history:

Often, I cannot explain a certain move, only know that it feels right, and it seems that my intuition is right more often than not. If I study a position for an hour, then I am usually going in loops and I'm probably not going to come up with something useful. I usually know what I am going to do after 10 seconds; the rest is double-checking.

Here is what Pamela Bingham, Managing Director, Rotork Gears, Leeds, Great Britain, is experiencing with the practice of Transcendental Meditation:

Meditation allows us to develop a state of "alert expectancy," which increases intuition and opportunity. The silence allows us to recognize our own intuition amidst the everyday distractions.

---

[5] Rosenthal (2011, p. 226).

[6] Harung & Travis (2016, p. 22).

[7] Farndale (2013).

Improved Creativity

Another commonly reported benefit of Transcendental Meditation is greater creativity. Creativity is known to follow four steps: Preparation, incubation, illumination, and expression. Transcending especially facilitates the incubation and illumination stages of creativity. You become more familiar with the silence at the source of thought that is the arena of creative insight.

Alpha1 EEG is reported during creative thinking and when solving a puzzle by insight.[8] Alpha1 EEG also accompanies the transformation from an ordinary solution to a novel and original one.[9]

Transcendental Meditation increases the presence of alpha1 EEG and is reported to increase creativity. The first study that Fred conducted reported higher scores on *Torrance Tests of Creative Thinking* in college students randomly assigned to learn TM.[10] Later, Fred showed that in 21 successful product development engineers at the car manufacturer Volvo in Sweden, there was a correlation between higher flexibility and originality in creativity tests and higher levels of brain integration, and a sense of being in control of one's situation.[11]

General Improvement from TM Practice

Researchers over the last 50 years report that regular practice of the Transcendental Meditation technique has a broad range of specific benefits: Increased intelligence, increased ability to learn and remember, increased self-development (the way we look upon ourselves, others, and the world), faster reaction time, reduced anxiety and stress, substantial improvements in health, greater calm, faster information processing, improved performance, and more.[12] For more details about this research, please refer to Chapter 7 where we summarized two major longitudinal studies on health and self-development. In a nutshell, an integrated brain will benefit anyone.

We can now appreciate why world-class performers like Ray Dalio, Ellen DeGeneres, Tom Hanks, David Lynch, Sir Paul McCartney, Gwyneth Paltrow, Sir Ringo Starr, Jerry Seinfeld, Howard Stern, and Oprah Winfrey all have enjoyed the many benefits of the Transcendental Meditation technique.[13]

Barry Zito[14] is a former American professional baseball player who made the American League All-Star team three times and won the Cy Young Award. When

---

[8] Cao et al. (2015).

[9] Schwab et al. (2014).

[10] Travis (1979).

[11] Travis & Lagrosen (2014).

[12] Maharishi International University (2023).

[13] Rosenthal (2011), Roth (2018).

[14] Rosenthal (2016, p. 101).

asked if his TM practice had helped him get into the zone and succeed in baseball, Barry replied:

> Yes, absolutely. Mastering yourself is what it's all about when you're out there on the field and managing all the distractions. … And TM for me is a really great practice because it allows me to become familiar with being quiet internally, and being in the present moment…

Ultimately, the greatest benefit of the Transcendental Meditation technique is peak experiences and the gradual growth to higher states of consciousness. This is our main interest. We found that the top-performing subjects in our studies tended to have peak experiences, the musicians in particular. Their many spontaneous peak experiences show that higher consciousness is completely natural. Having an integrated brain can change your experience of yourself and your relationship to the world. The promise, as shown by Fred's study[15] on those who had been practicing the TM technique for an average of 24 years, is a life lived with a profoundly different awareness—lasting peak experience and permanent inner bliss as one's normal awareness.

This is growth of higher states of consciousness. The inner wakefulness and expanded vision, initially experienced during Transcendental Meditation practice, is now the stable basis for life. You perceive the world as before—but not as before. Now, changing perceptions and feelings are appreciated on a non-changing screen of inner wakefulness. The next chapter explores higher states of consciousness.

References

Cao, Z., Li, Y., Hitchman, G., Qiu, J., & Zhang, Q. (2015). Neural correlates underlying insight problem solving: Evidence from EEG alpha oscillations. *Experimental Brain Research, 233*, 2497–2506. https://doi.org/10.1007/s00221-015-4338-1

Dawson, A. (2016, June 3). Why filmmaker David Lynch says Transcendental Meditation is the secret to success. *Los Angeles Times*.

Dillbeck, M. C., & Orme-Johnson, D. W. (1987). Physiological differences between Transcendental Meditation and rest. *American Psychologist, 42*(9), 879–881.

Farndale, N. (2013, October 19). Magnus Carlsen: Grandmaster flash. *Observer*.

Harung, H. S., & Travis, F. (2016). *Excellence through mind-brain development: The secrets of world-class performers*. Routledge.

Maharishi International University. (2023). Overview of research on Transcendental Meditation. TM Research Overview | Research (miu.edu). https://research.miu.edu/tm-technique/. Retrieved July 28, 2024.

Maharishi Mahesh Yogi. ([1963] 2001). *Science of being and art of living: Transcendental meditation*. Revised and updated edition. Plume (a member of Penguin Putnam).

Rosenthal, N. (2011). *Transcendence: Healing and transformation through transcendental meditation*. Jeremy P. Tarcher/Penguin.

Rosenthal, N. (2016). *Super mind: How to boost performance and live a richer and happier life through transcendental meditation*. Penguin Random House.

Roth, B. (2018). *Strength in stillness: The power of transcendental meditation*. Simon & Schuster.

---

[15] Travis et al. (2004).

Schwab, D., Benedek, M., Papousek, I., Weiss, E. M., & Fink, A. (2014). The time-course of EEG alpha power changes in creative ideation. *Frontiers in Human Neuroscience, 8*, 1–8. https://doi.org/10.3389/fnhum.2014.00310

Travis, F. T. (1979). The transcendental meditation technique and creativity: A longitudinal study of Cornell University undergraduates. *The Journal of Creative Behavior, 13*(3), 169–181.

Travis, F., Arenander, A., & DuBois, D. (2004). Psychological and physiological characteristics of a proposed object-referral/self-referral continuum of self-awareness. *Consciousness and Cognition, 13*(2), 401–420.

Travis, F., & Lagrosen, Y. (2014). Creativity and brain-functioning in product development engineers: A canonical correlation analysis. *Creativity Research Journal, 26*(2), 239–243.

Travis, F., & Parim, N. (2017). Default mode network activation and transcendental meditation practice: Focused attention or automatic self-transcending? *Brain and Cognition, 111*, 86–94.

Chapter 9
Peak Experiences and Higher States of Consciousness

Abstract We give an overview of the full range of human development and how this affects the quality of our life and our performance. First, we examine the developmental range described by modern science, culminating in Abraham Maslow's concept of self-actualization. Second, beyond this we describe four higher states of consciousness as defined by Maharishi Mahesh Yogi based on the ancient Vedic knowledge of India.

This chapter will consider two ranges of human development. First, the changes resulting from regular transcending, as reported in the previous chapter, will gradually lead to a better life, including less stress, more happiness, better health, and higher performance. This growth culminates in self-actualization, which is normally considered the endpoint of human development in modern science. Abraham Maslow[1] observed that most people are dependent on others for satisfying such basic needs as safety, belongingness, and respect. In contrast, self-actualizers are far less dependent and far more growth-motivated, autonomous, and self-directed.

Second, there are also prospects of a more wide-reaching, fundamental shift to lasting peak experiences and happiness. This transformation to higher states of consciousness adds a new dimension to living life.

The peak experiences from top performers—which we've so far shared with you—often provide glimpses of this transformed reality. These descriptions frequently include intense happiness, the experience of time changing, an expanded sense of self, a feeling of witnessing or being detached from what's happening, and a sense of unity of existence.

In this chapter we'll go deeper into peak experiences, a term originally coined by Abraham Maslow, who observed that only one such experience could have wide-reaching, positive influences on a person's life.[2]

---

[1] Maslow (1968, 1971).

[2] Ibid.

© The Author(s), under exclusive license to Springer Nature Switzerland AG 2025
H. S. Harung and F. Travis, *World-Class Brain*,
https://doi.org/10.1007/978-3-031-86667-8_9

Maslow's Self-Actualization

Abraham Maslow investigated more than 100 highly accomplished people such as Albert Einstein, William James, Albert Schweitzer, Eleanor Roosevelt, and Benedict Spinoza. He called these people self-actualizers. These people have a special liking for privacy, for detachment, and for meditation. In his book *Toward A Psychology Of Being*, Maslow[3] describes self-actualized people:

> Self-actualizing people, those who have come to a high level of maturation, health, and self-fulfillment, have so much to teach us that sometimes they seem almost like a different breed of human beings. But, because it is so new, the exploration of the highest reaches of human nature and of its ultimate possibilities and aspirations is a difficult and tortuous task. It has involved for me the continuous destruction of cherished axioms, the perpetual coping with seeming paradoxes, contradictions and vaguenesses and the occasional collapse around my ears of long established, firmly believed in, and seemingly unassailable laws of psychology.

Maslow[4] noted that self-actualizers have a higher frequency of peak experiences in life, experiences which he called "moments of highest happiness and fulfillment." These experiences are described as moments of transcendence, wholeness, pure delight, becoming fully human, and beyond words. Maslow writes about peaks:

> ...it looks as if there were a single ultimate value for mankind, a far goal toward which all men strive. ... Heaven, so to speak, lies waiting for us through life ...

Ragnhild Boes[5] led the content analysis of our interviews with the world-class athletes and their controls. The analysis found that the top performers were characterized by significantly greater wholeness, self-reliance, and growth-orientation—all qualities that reflect a mature psychology in the direction of self-actualization.

Vedic Tradition of Knowledge in India

While self-actualizing people today might seem a breed apart, the understanding of peak experiences and higher human development is ancient and well-known in the subjective tradition of knowledge in India, called the *Vedic* tradition. "Veda" simply means knowledge. While Western science looks outside to investigate objects, the individuals in the Vedic tradition looked *inside* to probe the nature of thought and discover who we are at our fundamental basis.

Maharishi Mahesh Yogi—world-leading expert on higher human development—described a system of higher states of consciousness from the Vedic tradition. In addition, he brought out the Transcendental Meditation technique to cultivate growth to higher states of consciousness.

---

[3] Maslow (1968, pp. 71–72).

[4] Ibid., pp. 69, 153, 154.

[5] Boes et al. (2014).

The power of Transcendental Meditation to develop the person can be seen in Fred's study[6] comparing a group of (1) non-meditating individuals, (2) those practicing TM for an average of 7 years, and (3) those practicing TM for an average of 24 years. He not only measured their brain waves but also used structured interviews to assess their inner experiences. One question Fred asked was simply, "How would you describe yourself?".

Those who hadn't yet learned the Transcendental Meditation technique said things such as, "I kind of like to forge my own way." Or "I guess I'm open to new experiences, and I tend to appreciate those things that are different." These are healthy descriptions of sense of self. But notice they are in terms of their personality and how they behave in the world.

In contrast, the long-term meditators, who had much higher levels of brain integration (see Fig. 7.1), described themselves fundamentally differently, saying things such as:

> We ordinarily think of our self as this age; this color of hair; these hobbies. My experience is that my Self is a lot larger than that. It's immeasurably vast on a physical level. It is not just restricted to this physical environment.

Another long-term meditator said:

> My self is the "I am-ness." It's my Being. There's just a channel underneath that's just underlying everything. It's my essence there and it just doesn't stop where I stop. ... by "I," I mean this 5 ft. 2 [158 cm] person who moves around here and there.

Notice that the descriptions of sense of self by the non-meditating individuals have a completely different character than those by the long-term meditators.

Higher Self and Lower Self

As a basis for understanding the two above classes of experiences, let's consider how Maharishi[7] describes two levels of sense of self as the "lower self" and the "higher Self":

> Self has two connotations: Lower self and higher Self. The lower self is that aspect of the personality which deals only with the relative aspect of existence. It comprises the mind that thinks, the intellect that decides, the ego that experiences. This lower self functions only in the relative states of existence — waking, dreaming and deep sleep. ... The higher Self is that aspect of the personality which never changes, absolute Being, which is the very basis of the entire field of relativity, including the lower self.

Maharishi equates the higher Self with Being. This is the experience of our universal nature underlying thought and feelings. This may be the same level of life that

---

[6] Travis et al., (2004, p. 409).

[7] Maharishi (1969, p. 339).

Einstein (Chapter 1) referred to when he used the term "being" and Maslow when he wrote about "Being".[8]

As seen, the descriptions of the self of the non-meditating subjects were of their lower self. They described their self in terms of their personality and their changing experience. In contrast, the long-term meditators did not define themselves in terms of their personality or in terms of their thoughts or emotional state. They described a reality that is greater than their body—indeed they appear to be describing a reality that is underlying the body and individual activity, i.e., in the direction of the higher Self.

Model of Higher Consciousness

Maharishi[9] articulated a model of higher consciousness that places the higher Self in relation to waking, dreaming, and sleeping. This comprehensive model of the full range of human growth is not found in modern psychological and developmental theory.

This comprehensive model defines four higher states of consciousness beyond waking, sleeping, and dreaming. Each state is characterized by different subjective experiences and by different brain wave signatures. Peak experiences may be glimpses of optimal waking functioning or one of these higher states. Let's take a more detailed look at these higher states. We have used quotations from Maharishi to give a flavor of each state.

Fourth State: Transcendental Consciousness

The first higher state is Transcendental Consciousness. Maharishi[10] describes Transcendental Consciousness as the state when the mind is completely settled:

This is a state of inner wakefulness with no object of thought or perception, just pure consciousness aware of its own unbounded nature.

Transcendental Consciousness is the individual's direct experience of this expanded and non-localized underlying field of pure consciousness or Being, which is the common basis of all individuals.

Fred[11] asked students to describe their deepest experiences during Transcendental Meditation practice. A content analysis of their descriptions yielded three themes that were common to all reports—absence of time, absence of space, and absence

---

[8] Maslow (1968).

[9] Alexander et al. (1990).

[10] Maharishi (1976, p. 123).

[11] Travis & Pearson (2000).

of body sense. Time, space, and body sense are the framework that gives meaning to waking experience. Note that Transcendental Consciousness was not described in terms of distorted content—strong emotions, or vivid visual, auditory, and tactile sensations, or distorted sense of self. Rather, Transcendental Consciousness was described by the absence of the customary framework and characteristics that define waking experience, as noted above.

Physiologically, Transcendental Consciousness is characterized by alpha1 brain coherence. This we have already explored in detail. Also, during these deep inner experiences, breath rate slows down and is often exceptionally slow.

Unified field. So far, we have discussed consciousness with respect to our mind. But where does matter fit into our model? Albert Einstein postulated that there is a unified state at the basis of the vast multiplicity of the physical universe. Today, quantum physicist John Hagelin writes that this fundamental state in physics is known as the *unified field*.[12] Physics describes the behavior of the unified field in terms of mathematical equations.

But where does consciousness fit into the picture? The meditation techniques of the Vedic tradition allow us to identify with and thereby know the essential nature of our individual consciousness, which as seen above is experienced as pure, unbounded consciousness. Based on Vedic Science, Maharishi[13] explained that everything in the universe is ultimately this pure, unbounded consciousness. All that exists in the universe—mind and matter—is ultimately the unified field of consciousness. The physical world is therefore an expression of consciousness, as Maharishi has said[14]:

> When we consider the relationship between the objective and subjective values of creation, we find that the objective value is just the projection of consciousness …

Likewise, several leading physicists have argued that consciousness is fundamental to matter. For example, the German physicist Max Planck,[15] who discovered the quantized nature of the subatomic world, said:

> I regard consciousness as primary. I regard matter as a derivative of consciousness.

In an article in *Scientific American*, the French physicist Bernard d'Espagnat[16] writes that the doctrine that the world is made up of objects whose existence is independent of human consciousness turns out to be in conflict with quantum mechanics and with the facts established by experiment.

The idea that consciousness is basic is also supported by many scientists from other sciences. The Harvard and MIT trained expert on human physiology and consciousness Dr. Tony Nader describes the universe as the expression of consciousness in his ground-breaking book *Consciousness Is All There Is: How Understanding and Experiencing Consciousness Will Transform Your Life*.[17]

---

[12] Hagelin (1987).

[13] Maharishi (1976, 1978).

[14] Maharishi (1978, p. 94).

[15] Quoted in: Klein (1984).

[16] d'Espagnat (1979).

[17] Nader (2024).

The 2022 article in *Scientific American* by neurologist Christopher Walsh[18] asks, "What are the roots of consciousness?" and questions whether it is possible that consciousness can be mediated by "a bunch of cells and chemicals." The Norwegian book, *Reality is Larger: A Holistic Paradigm*, by Dag Andersen, reviews a wide range of multidisciplinary research supporting an underlying field of consciousness.[19]

Fifth State: Cosmic Consciousness

The fifth state of consciousness grows by alternating the experience of Transcendental Consciousness with waking activity. This state, called Cosmic Consciousness, is the integration of deep inner transcendence with waking, dreaming, and sleeping. In Cosmic Consciousness, the physical rest during sleep, the illusory dream images, and the changing waking experiences come and go on a continuum of inner self-awareness. Immovable inner silence and ever-changing outer activity are together in one awareness. Inner silence is the background for the flux of ongoing outer experiences. This coexistence of inner silence and outer activity is called "witnessing." Maharishi[20] describes Cosmic Consciousness in this way:

> Then a man realizes that his Self is different from the mind which is engaged with thoughts and desires. It is now his experience that the mind, which had been identified with desires, is mainly identified with the Self. He experiences the desires of the mind as lying outside himself, whereas he used to experience himself as completely involved with desires. On the surface of the mind desires certainly continue, but deep within the mind they no longer exist, for the depths of the mind are transformed into the nature of the Self. All the desires which were present in the mind have been thrown upward, as it were — they have gone to the surface, and within the mind the finest intellect gains an unshakeable, immovable status.

Notice that the key characteristic of Cosmic Consciousness is the coexistence of inner immovable silence along with ongoing mental activity and behavior.

Physiologically, the state of Cosmic Consciousness is characterized by the coexistence of alpha1 brain waves (seen during Transcendental Meditation practice) with the EEG of sleep[21] (delta waves) and the EEG of cognitive processing while awake[22] (beta and gamma waves). The co-existence of these brain waves supports the subjective reports that the experience of Transcendental Consciousness coexists with waking, dreaming, and sleeping.

Glimpses of higher states of consciousness from our world-class performers. The subjects in our three peak performance studies reported a wide range of enhanced experiences during activity that in some cases indicates higher consciousness, including greatly expanded awareness; a feeling that everything is right; effortless

---

[18] Walsh (2022).

[19] Andersen (2020).

[20] Maharishi (1969, pp. 150–151).

[21] Mason et al. (1997).

[22] Travis et al. (2002).

and automatic action; frequent luck; and intense inner happiness.[23] To illustrate, the following description of optimal performance by the world-class handball goalkeeper Heidi Tjugum (See Chapter 4) sounds like an experience of Cosmic Consciousness:

> Sometimes I have felt that I am an observer — I just watch what happens. This is a good feeling; it is a very beautiful feeling; it is not that I feel I don't have control. But it goes by itself — in reality I do not have to initiate anything at all. Extremely here and now — nothing else matters. And it is unbelievably good. Beautiful experience. These feelings are unbelievably nice. They stimulate me to taking on further challenges. Obviously, this is what I am longing for every time I go to a training session.

Fortunately, science has now shown that this exalted state of awareness isn't something imagined but is a natural experience that results from specific changes in brain functioning. In both the top performers and the long-term meditators, that change involves the greater presence of the alpha1 coherence of silence alongside the EEG of active thinking and interacting with the environment. Thus, science has now explained what the masters from the Vedic tradition have known to be the case for thousands of years—the coexistence of silence and dynamism.

Sixth State: Refined Cosmic Consciousness

We've now looked at the fifth state of consciousness, Cosmic Consciousness. So, what about the sixth state? Whereas Cosmic Consciousness entails a fundamental shift in our inner experience of the Self, Refined Cosmic Consciousness entails a fundamental shift in and refinement of our perception of the surroundings. Maharishi[24] describes this state as follows:

> In the fifth state of consciousness, where the fourth state of consciousness has come to be coexistent with the waking state of consciousness, the perception is of the surface value of objects. And when the perception becomes so refined that it is able to perceive the finest relative on the surface of the grossest relative, then this will certainly be another state of consciousness distinctly different in its characteristics than the fifth state of consciousness: the unbounded awareness with the ability of perception of the finest relative. We have the right to say a sixth state of consciousness. … This is developed by continued alternation of the fourth state of consciousness with more refined activity which is guided by the impulse of the heart — activity guided more by feeling.

Seventh State: Unity Consciousness

Beyond Refined Cosmic Consciousness is Unity Consciousness, in which one experiences everything in life—mental and physical—in terms of the unified field of consciousness, as defined earlier in this chapter.

---

[23] Harung (2012).

[24] Maharishi (1972, lesson 23).

Maharishi[25] describes Unity Consciousness as a state "where form is cognized as non-form." The hidden, transcendental aspect of the object comes up on the surface, and the object is experienced in its infinite value—in terms of the Self. In this highest state of consciousness, harmony dominates—the cognition of the infinite value of life becomes primary, even as one continues to perceive the innumerable differences on the more surface levels of life. Maharishi describes this state as follows[26]:

> The seventh state of consciousness, we may very well call unified state of consciousness, where the ultimate value of the object, the infinite, unmanifest, ultimate value of the object breathes life, or becomes lively.

Here's one of Fred's[27] subjects who reported having Unity experiences. She answered the question, "How would you describe yourself?" this way:

> I look out and see this beautiful ... intelligence ... you could say in the sky, in the tree, but really being expressed through these things ... and these [things] are my Self.

In our research, the professional viola player Birgitta J. Halbakken[28] of the Oslo Philharmonic Orchestra describes an inner experience in the direction of Unity Consciousness:

> This state can occur when I play a concert. In my case it can be described as if my inner expands to include the activity of the whole orchestra and even the audience. ... A quivering pleasurable sensation at the same time as a total focus is on the activity. The mind doesn't just listen, but is a part of the music, which together with space, audience, co-players, and conductor become a wholeness.

The 5th, 6th, and 7th states of consciousness are collectively known as *enlightenment*. Enlightenment is associated with a deep sense of inner peace and bliss. Suffering is a thing of the past. The Vedic tradition maintains that these higher states are the birthright of everyone, and that it is simply a matter of systematically cultivating one's awareness through transcending and contacting pure consciousness, and then engaging in daily activity to stabilize this holistic growth.

* * *

We've discussed a wide range of topics so far in this short book, from the brain waves of world-class athletes to the blissful experiences of Unity Consciousness. But there's one more important point beyond this apex of higher states of individual consciousness: The creation of greater coherence in the organizations where we work and the society within which we live.

For us as the authors of this book, the benefit of an integrated brain goes beyond the benefit for the individual. Research suggests that people with the sort of coherent brains we've been discussing will automatically create a harmonious effect in their

---

[25] Katz (2011, p. 328).

[26] Maharishi (1972, lesson 23).

[27] Travis et al., (2004, p. 409).

[28] Harung & Travis (2016, p. 83).

environment—without even intending to. It's a big claim that goes beyond the current prevalent world view. However, in the next two chapters we use research to show that it's a very reasonable claim.

References

Alexander, C., Davies, J., Dixon, C. A., Dillbeck, M., Druker, S., Oetzel, R. M., Muehlman, J. M., & Orme-Johnson, D. (1990). Growth of higher stages of consciousness: Maharishi Vedic Psychology of human development. In C. N. Alexander & E. Langer (Eds.), *Higher stages of human development* (pp. 259–341). Oxford University Press.

Andersen, D. (2020). *Virkeligheten er Større: Et Holistisk Paradigme (Reality is larger: A holistic paradigm)* (p. 122). Elvehøy, Oslo.

Boes, R., Harung, H. S., Travis, F., & Pensgaard, A. M. (2014). Mental and physical attributes defining world-class Norwegian athletes: Content analysis of interviews. *Scandinavian Journal of Medicine and Science in Sports, 24,* 422–427.

d'Espagnat, B. (1979, November). The quantum theory and reality. *Scientific American.*

Hagelin, J. S. (1987). Is consciousness the unified field? A field theorist's perspective. *Modern Science and Vedic Science, 1*(1), 29–88.

Harung, H. S. (2012). Illustrations of peak experiences during optimal performance in world-class performers: Integrating Eastern and Western insights. *Journal of Human Values, 18*(1), 33–52.

Harung, H. S., & Travis, F. (2016). *Excellence through mind-brain development: The secrets of world-class performers.* Routledge.

Katz, V. (2011). *Conversations with Maharishi,* Vol. 1. Maharishi International University Press. www.miupress.org.

Klein, D. B. (1984). *The conception of consciousness: A survey.* University of Nebraska Press.

Maharishi Mahesh Yogi. (1969). *On the Bhagavad-Gita: A new translation and commentary,* Chapters 1–6. Penguin.

Maharishi Mahesh Yogi. (1972). *The science of creative intelligence: Knowledge and experience.* [Syllabus of videotaped course]. Maharishi International University Press.

Maharishi Mahesh Yogi. (1976). *Creating an ideal society.* MERU Press Publication 1530.

Maharishi Mahesh Yogi. (1978). *Enlightenment to every individual, invincibility to every nation.* Maharishi European Research University Press Publication G 1530. Printed in West Germany by MERU Press.

Maslow, A. H. (1968). *Toward a psychology of being* (2nd ed.). Van Nostrand Reinhold.

Maslow, A. H. (1971). *The farther reaches of human nature.* The Viking Press.

Mason, L. I., Alexander, C. N., Travis, F. T., Marsh, G., Orme-Johnson, D. W., Gackenbach, J., Mason, D. C., Rainforth, M., & Walton, K. G. (1997). Electrophysiological correlates of higher states of consciousness during sleep in long-term practitioners of the Transcendental Meditation program. *Sleep, 20*(2), 102–110.

Nader, T. (2024). *Consciousness is all there is: How understanding and experiencing consciousness will transform your life.* Hay House.

Travis, F., & Pearson, C. (2000). Pure consciousness: Distinct phenomenological and physiological correlates of "consciousness itself." *The International Journal of Neuroscience, 100,* 1–10.

Travis, F., Tecce, J., Arenander, A., & Wallace, R. K. (2002). Patterns of EEG coherence, power, and contingent negative variation characterize the integration of transcendental and waking states. *Biological Psychology, 61,* 293–319.

Travis, F., Arenander, A., & DuBois, D. (2004). Psychological and physiological characteristics of a proposed object-referral/self-referral continuum of self-awareness. *Consciousness and Cognition, 13*(2), 401–420.

Walsh, C. (2022, September). Revealing the genes that shape the human brain. *Scientific American.*

Chapter 10
From Integrated Brains to Integrated Organizations

Abstract The quality of the members of an organization is the major determinant of its overall performance. As an organization becomes more developed or integrated, that organization will display similar features to those seen in individuals with more integrated brain functioning: Coherence, wakefulness, and efficiency. Such development is illustrated by a few case studies of high-performing organizations.

The research on world-class performers that we've presented in this book shows they tend to have higher brain integration as measured by greater coherence, more wakefulness (as indicated by higher alpha1 power), and more efficient brain functioning. They also have higher levels of moral development and more frequent peak experiences. In addition, high brain connectivity has been shown to correlate with scoring high on favorable measures such as vocabulary, memory, life satisfaction, income, and years of education. To summarize, top performers are happier, more intelligent, and more effective.

But no person is an island. Our performance is affected by those around us. If you're around someone who's competent and upbeat, you'll typically feel better than when you're around someone who's struggling and depressed. One gives you energy; the other takes your energy. So, if you have many top performers in a community— each enjoying and radiating his or her special qualities—you might expect that there would then be greater coherence and performance in that community.

Features of More Advanced Organizations

To illustrate the features of more advanced organizations, let's consider how such organizations can express the three qualities we found in integrated brains: Coherence, wakefulness, and efficiency.

© The Author(s), under exclusive license to Springer Nature Switzerland AG 2025
H. S. Harung and F. Travis, *World-Class Brain*,
https://doi.org/10.1007/978-3-031-86667-8_10

1. **Coherence**. The book *Firms of Endearment: How World-class Companies Profit from Passion and Purpose*[1] describes many of the qualities of advanced companies. Traditionally, the focus in the business world has been only or mainly on maximizing the return on investment for the business owners—the shareholders. In contrast, an increasing number of companies like 3M, BMW, IKEA, Johnson & Johnson, Southwest Airlines, Tomra Systems,[2] and Toyota seem to have the desire and ability to satisfy all stakeholders: Associates, customers, shareholders, business partners, and society. They align associates through a shared and lively vision for the future, a core purpose, and a set of core values. Such companies work like an integrated brain, where *all* parts—though performing different tasks—are working in synergy for the common good.

   If you're the CEO of a company, is it really possible to look after your employees and nourish your business partners at the same time that you are running the business in a successful way? Yes, these firms pay their associates well. Yes, they do not squeeze their suppliers. Yes, they contribute to society. In spite of all this, it turns out that in terms of return on investment to the shareholders, in the US the public firms of endearment outperformed the Standard & Poor 500 companies by more than 8-to-1 over a 10-year period. This illustrates the power of creating coherence among diverse activities and establishing win-win relations.

   We saw in Chapter 3 that nations characterized by more equality are healthier and happier. Perhaps the same applies to organizations?

2. **Wakefulness and inner-directedness**. A study[3] by the Korn/Ferry Institute suggests that greater inner-centered awareness among the members of an organization translates into higher collective performance. The study found higher financial performance in companies where the associates were more aware of their own strengths and weaknesses and had a greater tendency to reflect. These companies significantly outperformed those businesses where these features were less prominent.

3. **Efficiency**. The shared peak experiences that we'll now present illustrate the efficient functioning of advanced organizations.

Shared Peak Experiences

Previously in this book we have presented a number of uplifting individual peak experiences that often are related to peak performance. As individuals have their level of mind-brain development, so a collection of individuals has an overall level of functioning that could be called the *collective consciousness*.[4] The collective

---

[1] Sisodia et al. (2014).

[2] A Norwegian company that is a world leader in recycling.

[3] Zes & Landis (2013).

[4] Maharishi (1976).

consciousness is a characteristic of any group of people, such as a family, team, organization, community, country, or the whole world. In this chapter we'll focus on the collective consciousness of organizations and in the next on this shared reality of society.

This quote from Anna Skogman,[5] a professional violin player in the Norwegian Opera, gives an example of a shared peak experience, which illustrates collective consciousness functioning at a high level:

> Sometimes during a performance [in an orchestra]… you can feel that everybody is focused; it becomes easy, as if all of us suddenly became one body where all the parts are working perfectly together, everybody breathes together, everything becomes one big energy, and everything feels crystal clear, like the brains/souls of everybody melt together and want the same. It doesn't matter if you play the oboe or triangle, or conduct. … I feel a direct mental connection with both any co-musicians and members of the audience. A very real contact. However, I'm thinking very little about the others in the room. (Thoughts that otherwise can be present: "Do they like what I'm doing?" and performance anxiety, etc. are totally gone.) The only thing that is important is the music. Who is there, and what they are, think of me — everything like that disappears. I only feel their and my own mental presence.

The qualities of coherence, wakefulness, and efficiency are all evident from "as if all of us suddenly became one body where all the parts are working perfectly together, everybody breathes together, everything becomes one big energy, and everything feels crystal clear, like the brains/souls of everybody melt together and want the same."

The handball player Susann Goksør Bjerkrheim in our research was part of the Norwegian national women's handball team that won one gold, one silver, and one bronze in world championships, two silver and one bronze in the Olympic Games, and one silver and one bronze in European championships. In what seems to be a *collective peak experience*, Susann[6] describes an experience she had several times when playing for various teams:

> Sometimes, all the way from the warmup the communication with the other team members is good, and you know in advance that today you are going to succeed in an unbelievable way. On such days, there is a shared, positive mood in the team. It is abstract and gives energy. I feel the response from others. Everybody is fully present in the situation. There is a mass suggestive effect where we all melt into a greater fellowship. I get chills down my spine. I feel world-class when this community mood is there — a strong togetherness or coherence. During such exhilarated times, when things fall into place … the action of each player is extremely well coordinated with those of all the other players. There is rhythm and harmony in the team. We read each other correctly, things float, and there is a high spirit and energy. Everybody contributes her energy into the team. Definitely extreme energy is created.

Again, the three qualities are expressed:

1. **Coherence**: "… the communication with the other team members is good …", "… we all melt into a greater fellowship," and "I feel world-class when this community mood is there—a strong togetherness or coherence."

---

[5] Harung & Travis (2016, pp. 113–114).

[6] Harung (2012).

2. *Wakefulness*: "Everybody is fully present in the situation," and "We read each other correctly, things float, and there is a high spirit and energy."
3. *Efficiency*: "During such exhilarated times, when things fall into place ... the action of each player is extremely well coordinated with those of all the other players."

Interestingly, research[7] on flow suggests that "when a team experiences flow collectively the experience is far more satisfying than it is when each member experiences it individually." We expect the same to be the case for peak experiences.

Notice how Anna Skogman above is speaking about experiencing a shared reality among everyone present when she reports, "I feel a direct mental connection with both any co-musicians and members of the audience." Now we'll examine how we can raise the level of this shared reality.

How to Enhance Collective Consciousness

Let's consider how a few members developing their own brain and mind can raise the collective consciousness of an organization, which we may call *organizational consciousness*. Many corporations have introduced Transcendental Meditation to their associates, and research has been conducted to assess the results. Fortunately, it seems that even a relatively small portion of the members practicing this technique will cause overall growth of organizational collective consciousness.[8] More research is needed to establish the relationship between organizational size and the critical minimum number of meditators. However, it seems that the larger the organization, the smaller is the threshold percentage. For the larger social units of cities, the threshold is as low as 1%, as we shall see in the next chapter. In the following, we'll also mention research on individual benefits that can help explain the corporate benefits.

Nordic Naturals. Nordic Naturals in Watsonville, California is a leading global manufacturer and distributor of omega 3 products, with around 50% of the market in the US. Out of the close to 200 associates at the headquarters in Watsonville, more than 70 have so far chosen to learn the Transcendental Meditation technique, i.e., over 1/3 of the associates. The company pays for the instruction and there is a meditation room available. The sales of Nordic Naturals are growing well over 10% each year, while the omega 3 oil industry as a whole normally is growing at about 1.5% annually.

H. A. Montgomery. A Detroit chemical-manufacturing company, H. A. Montgomery, made it possible for the associates to learn and practice the Transcendental Meditation technique. The company experienced dramatic benefits when 52 out of its 70 workers practiced this technique twice daily. Absenteeism fell 85%, injuries

---

[7] Fabritius & Hagemann (2017, p. 267).

[8] Gustavsson (1992).

fell 70%, sick days dropped 76%, productivity increased 120%, quality control rose 240%, and profits increased as much as 520%.[9]

Lindsey Adelman. Lindsey Adelman runs a New York and Los Angeles business that manufactures and sells artistic chandeliers.[10] Her company subsidized 40 associates learning the TM technique. She observes:

> It has made a difference with the success for big-picture reasons that are quite specific, like employee retention — which is very high. I think that has a lot to do with our success as a company. ... Everyone's taking on different responsibilities; everyone's redefining their jobs; everyone has a deeper understanding of my vision for the future. ... And I'm really proud of our interpersonal relationships. I think that also has a lot to do with people practicing TM.

Bridgewater Associates. Bridgewater Associates in Connecticut, USA—one of the world's largest hedge funds—provides another example of how Transcendental Meditation is increasingly being used in the corporate world to increase creativity, reduce stress, and improve performance. Founder Ray Dalio has practiced this technique for over 50 years. In an article[11] stating that Transcendental Meditation is "taking over Wall Street," Ray calls this technique "the single biggest influence" on his life. The article continues:

> Around eight years ago ... Ray Dalio introduced Transcendental Meditation to his then 735 employees. "I did it because it's the greatest gift I could give anyone — it brings about equanimity, creativity and peace." ... Since then, TM has popped into the mainstream, and over the last three years, the David Lynch Foundation TM center [in New York] has taught almost 2,500 professionals, with roughly 55% of those from Wall Street.

Norman Rosenthal[12] writes in his book *Super Mind* that Dalio subsidizes any associate who wants to learn the Transcendental Meditation technique.

Swedish study. An investigation in Sweden found that a group of meditating managers in a private business grew in holistic thinking and became more aware of the important issues facing the company, as assessed by a superior.[13]

* * *

This chapter has considered the development of integrated teams and organizations. As we saw in Chapter 6, we expect that the enhanced coherence and level of performance in teams and organizations is caused by an interaction of direct communication between people (hyperscanning) and the field effect of consciousness. For teams, families, and small organizations it seems likely that interactions involving speech and sight dominate in determining the level of coherence. In contrast, we think that the field effect of consciousness becomes increasingly important in determining the level of cooperation and quality of life as we move to larger and larger

---

[9] Aburdene (2007).

[10] Rosenthal (2016, p. 189).

[11] Feloni (2016).

[12] Rosenthal (2016, p. 189).

[13] Gustavsson (1992).

collections of people, such as larger cities, nations, and the whole world. This will be the topic of the next chapter.

References

Aburdene, P. (2007). *Megatrends 2010: The rise of conscious capitalism.* Hampton Roads Publishing Company.

Fabritius, F., & Hagemann, H. W. (2017). *The leading brain: Powerful science-based strategies for achieving peak performance.* A TarcherPerigee Book.

Feloni, R. (2016). http://www.businessinsider.in/Transcendental-Meditation-which-Bridgewat ers-Ray-Dalio-calls-the-single-biggest-influence-on-his-life-is-taking-over-Wall-Street/articl eshow/55252426.cms. Retrieved July 25, 2024.

Gustavsson, B. (1992). *The transcendent organization.* PhD Dissertation, Department of Business Administration, University of Stockholm, Sweden.

Harung, H. S. (2012). Illustrations of peak experiences during optimal performance in world-class performers: Integrating Eastern and Western insights. *Journal of Human Values, 18*(1), 33–52.

Harung, H. S., & Travis, F. (2016). *Excellence through mind-brain development: The secrets of world-class performers.* Routledge.

Maharishi Mahesh Yogi. (1976). *Creating an ideal society.* MERU Press Publication 1530, Rheinweiler, West Germany.

Rosenthal, N. (2016). *Super mind: How to boost performance and live a richer and happier life through transcendental meditation.* Penguin Random House.

Sisodia, R., Sheth, J. N., & Wolfe, D. B. (2014). *Firms of endearment: How world-class companies profit from passion and purpose*, 2nd ed. Pearson Education.

Zes, D., & Landis, D. (2013, August). A better return on self-awareness. Companies with higher rates of return on stock also have employees with fewer personal blind spots. Korn/Ferry Institute.

Chapter 11
From Integrated Brains to an Integrated Society

Abstract We consider the interaction between individual and collective consciousness—through an underlying field of consciousness—and research on raising collective consciousness towards an integrated society. Next, we propose that a "consciousness revolution" is currently taking place, and we quote a number of highly inspiring statistics suggesting that the world may be moving towards a golden age.

The Field Effect of Consciousness

We discussed in the previous chapter that in the same way that individual consciousness underlies individual thought and behavior, so there is a collective consciousness underlying the functioning of a collection of individuals, such as an organization or a society.[1] Below we'll consider further research demonstrating that this collective consciousness is an underlying *field* and that there's a "field effect" of consciousness. A field has *non-local* properties that influence events across space. It has with humor been said that if you tickle it here, it laughs over there.

The gravitational field extends throughout the universe and keeps planets and galaxies in their orbit—and our feet on the ground. Through the electromagnetic field, we can use our mobile phone to reach our friends all over the world. Instantaneously.

We generally think of consciousness as being localized in people's brains. That is individual conscious experience, which is very dependent on brain functioning. But at the same time a non-local field of consciousness exists, called pure consciousness, which we discussed in Chapter 9. Pure consciousness underlies individual thoughts and actions. Individual consciousness reflects this universal field through the functioning of our brain. A good analogy would be the way a laptop transforms non-local Wi-Fi waves into tangible information. You will probably have noticed that wherever you move your laptop in the Wi-Fi field, all information is available, because in a field all information is everywhere.

Recall that both an increasing number of scholars in both modern science and ancient Vedic knowledge suggest that consciousness is a non-local field underlying

---

[1] Maharishi (1976).

© The Author(s), under exclusive license to Springer Nature Switzerland AG 2025
H. S. Harung and F. Travis, *World-Class Brain*,
https://doi.org/10.1007/978-3-031-86667-8_11

both mind and matter. This theory is supported by 28 empirical studies, published in peer-reviewed journals, reporting that the quality of life in society improves significantly because of groups of individuals practicing Transcendental Meditation, and in most studies also the advanced TM-Sidhi program (see below).[2] This improvement is a result of stimulating the universal, unified field of consciousness. However, through the internet and media, hyperscanning (Chapter 6) may also play a modest part in the improvement of human interaction on the social scale.

Research on the Field Effect of Consciousness

When Maharishi introduced Transcendental Meditation to the world in 1959, he said that there are not only individual benefits but also social benefits. In the mid-1970s some social scientists[3] looked at cities that had at least 1% of the population practicing Transcendental Meditation and found that crime rate went down as these cities reached that threshold. This was the first documented example that stirring the underlying field of consciousness through transcending could improve the behavior of the society as a whole.

The United States has about 320 million people. To get measurable improvements in the quality of life through 1% of the population practicing Transcendental Meditation, about 3.2 million people would need to practice this technique. That is a large number of people. But researchers discovered that the combined coherence of the Transcendental Meditation and TM-Sidhi programs is much more effective: It only takes the square root of 1% of the population to practice these techniques together in *one locality* to create measurable signs of positivity in society. For the US, that's a group of about 1700 people practicing the Transcendental Meditation and TM-Sidhi program together.

Many published studies have found that such coherence-creating groups facilitate reduced war intensity, reduced terrorism, reduced crime, fewer traffic accidents, and increased stock market indexes when the square root of 1% of the population in a country practices the Transcendental Meditation and TM-Sidhi programs together. For an overview of this research, please refer to two intriguing books[4] *The Field Paradigm: 20 Experiments That Can Change The World* and *An Antidote To Violence: Evaluating The Evidence*.

The first study[5] we'll refer to in detail is one that examined the effect of a series of seven assemblies within a 2 1/4-year period on reducing collective tension and violence and enhancing cooperative behavior among antagonistic parties in a war in the Middle East during the 1980s. Daily event data were derived from nine international and regional news sources. Levels of conflict, cooperation, and casualties

---

[2] Global Union of Scientists for Peace (2024).

[3] Dillbeck et al. (1981).

[4] Claes (2017), Spivack & Saunders (2020).

[5] Orme-Johnson et al. (1988), Davies & Alexander (2005).

were scored by an experienced local coder blind to the hypotheses and techniques employed. Statistical analysis of the data found an estimated mean 66% increase in cooperation and estimated reductions of 48% in conflict, 71% in war fatalities, and 68% in war injuries during the assemblies.

A second, more recent study found that over a period of four years, a group of at least 1700 in Fairfield, Iowa, the home of Maharishi International University, was able to decrease the number of homicides and violent crimes in the whole of the US. The experiment, which took place during 2007–2010, found that there were 8157 fewer homicides and 182,744 fewer violent crimes in the US than would have been predicted based on crime trends during the previous four years. Over this four-year period the homicide rate declined 21.2% and violent crime 18.5%.[6]

The above study was later expanded upon, finding the same level of temporary decline during the experimental period in eight US social variables: "… there were significant and meaningful trend reductions in indicators of national stress: Homicides, rape, aggravated assault, robbery, infant mortality, drug-related deaths, motor vehicle fatalities, fatalities due to injuries in youths ages 10–19, and in a composite index of all eight variables (p's < 0.0001)."[7]

The researchers looked at a wide range of alternative explanations, such as policing, demographic trends, and unemployment trends, but none could explain these reductions. Statistical analysis showed that the probability of these reductions happening by chance was very small: Less than 3 in 10,000 million million for homicide and less than 3 in 100 million for violent crime.

Now here's the thing: A relatively small group of people in and around Fairfield, Iowa, USA, were radiating an influence on the whole country. Earlier we speculated that top performers would naturally radiate a positive influence on those around them. But in this case, there was little contact between the group in Iowa and people around the nation. The group was in southeastern Iowa, and the changes were taking place nationwide in the US. How could that be? The only possible explanation is that there is a field effect of consciousness, as already described.

Interestingly, there are other examples in modern science illustrating that a small percentage of the individual elements in a system can create order in the whole system: "… a small number of coherent neurons in the brain leads to coherent brain activity and … a small number of coherently moving photons can induce all the other photons to become coherent, creating laser light."[8]

---

[6] Dillbeck & Cavanaugh (2016).

[7] Orme-Johnson et al. (2022).

[8] Nader (2024, p. 324).

Shifts in Collective Behavior Through Higher Collective Consciousness

When groups of people collectively contact pure consciousness during their TM and TM-Sidhi practice, they thrill this underlying field. Then this underlying field becomes more functionally significant in everyone's life. Theory and research[9] suggest that with higher coherence in the collective consciousness of society, there will be a shift towards more prevention; more win–win solutions; more inclusiveness; more happiness, love, and empathy; higher moral behavior; and more holistic solutions.

The related development of moral reasoning leads to a shift from narrow self-interest to an expanded concern for others and society. In fact, moral development has three major ranges: Egocentric, socio-centric, and world-centric.[10]

With such transformations, we would expect few problems and much higher performance, and thereby enhanced individual and collective success. The only thing the members of the coherence-creating group are doing is enjoying the bliss of their twice daily meditations. Therefore, this transformation is characterized by "doing less and accomplishing more," the central principle of economics, which is also a principle governing all natural processes in the physical world.[11]

Is a Consciousness Revolution Next?

The world is now enjoying the many benefits of the IT revolution. We are convinced that the next major global step will be the *consciousness revolution*. Only by individuals developing their consciousness will they be able to gain a global perspective. Raising collective consciousness requires enhanced levels of brain integration in society. Recall that individuals in our research with higher levels of brain integration were more successful and had higher moral reasoning.

When we talk about the ongoing shift to a fundamentally better society, we often meet skepticism based on the mounting environmental problems, including global warming. Of course, we need to control global warming and make our societies sustainable. However, our globe is receiving 11,000 times more energy from the sun than we as humans use.[12] The direct use of solar energy is accelerating, and its price is now on the same level as that of oil. The newspaper *Aftenposten* in Oslo printed a notice on the 30th of May 2017 that in Europe alone, close to 4.2 million people are now working to improve the environment.

---

[9] See for example: Harung (1999/2018), Harung & Travis (2016).

[10] Lawrence Kohlberg, quoted in: Wilber (2000, p. 45).

[11] Hagelin (1987).

[12] Trømborg (2017).

If we combine these factors, it seems likely that before long human creativity will have solved the problems with polluting fossil energy and global warming by extracting clean energy direct from the sun's rays. It is encouraging that according to a recent report by the *Global Electricity Review*, as referred to by CNN, "solar was the fastest-growing source of electricity in 2023 for the 19th consecutive year," which meant that a record-breaking 30% of the world's electricity was produced by renewables in this year.[13]

It is gratifying that today's people are much more concerned than before about sustainability and the whole world. This was illustrated by the climate meeting in Paris during the fall of 2015, which was closely followed by people from all over the world, and where the resolution was signed by more than 150 countries. The increasing concern for sustainability illustrates the growing world-centric awareness resulting from a rising world consciousness.

Evidence of Rising World Consciousness

Before we describe the extensive, fundamental improvements presently taking place in the world, let's establish that there is a huge potential for such development. In her doctoral dissertation at Harvard University, Susanne Cook-Greuter[14] estimated that only around 1% of the adult population in today's society reaches self-actualization, as described in Chapter 9.

Here are some illustrations[15] of the good news resulting from the present rising of world consciousness:

- The average lifespan globally has increased from 30 to 73 years from 1850 to today.
- The number of people in the world who die due to starvation has fallen by 98% over the last 100 years (while the world population has increased fourfold).
- Over the last 200 years, the share of the global population living in extreme poverty has declined from about 75% to about 10%.
- The World Bank projects that in less than 20 years, poverty could almost be eradicated from the world.
- The number of homicides per 100,000 people in Western Europe is approaching zero.
- We have more democracy. At the turn of the century, 140 out of the world's approximately 190 nations were democratic with functioning multiple party elections.
- We have a new system of international law.
- The rights of women and children have been strengthened.

---

[13] CNN (2023).

[14] Cook-Greuter (1999/2000).

[15] Pinker (2019), Rosling (2018), Moatsos (2021), Diaz (2014), Diamandis (2016), Ringen (2017), Gates (2018).

- In the last 25 years, mortality rates for children under five years of age have dropped by 50%.
- More than 90% of all children in the world now attend primary school.
- In the last 16 years, the number of children in hazardous work conditions and performing child labor has declined by more than 50%.

The major shift towards a fundamentally better world seems mainly to have started with the Industrial Revolution in England around 1800. Since then, there have been huge improvements, mainly in technology, but also in quality of life, as just illustrated. Admittedly, there have also been major setbacks on the way, notably the two world wars. And recently there have been setbacks in several of the above statistics due to the much smaller wars in Ukraine and the Middle East, and due to the pandemic. Fortunately, recently there are changes indicating that the world again is improving. For example, extreme poverty is now declining again, but it is estimated that it will take until 2024 to return to the 2019 levels.[16]

Thus overall, there has been extensive and continued progress. As J. Diaz[17] a few years ago concluded:

> While there's still plenty of war, hunger, sickness, and poverty in the world, things are much better than what they were only a few decades ago — not to talk about centuries ago. We are still far from utopia, but the data is stubborn: We are getting there. Fast.

It may be a challenge to imagine that the world now is changing for the better in a fundamental way. After all, the media has been feeding us with mainly negative news for years and years. Consequently, many people are surprised when they read about the positive developments just listed.

Fortunately, coherence-creating groups are now being established in many countries, notably India where the goal is to create a group of at least 9000 experts, which should be sufficient to create peace in the whole world.[18] As these groups grow, we anticipate that the rising global consciousness will facilitate much additional positive news, and that in the media and society at large there will be an increasing focus on, and acceptance of, news of more peace, happiness, and prosperity in the world.

* * *

As seen in this chapter, we now have available efficient techniques to raise the collective consciousness of society and extensively speed up progress. On this basis, Maharishi[19] inaugurated a new golden age for the world back in 1975:

> Through the window of Science we see the dawn of the Age of Enlightenment. ... I am only giving expression to the phenomenon that is taking place.

---

[16] Nature (2023).

[17] Diaz (2014).

[18] Global Union of Scientists for Peace (2024).

[19] Maharishi International University (1975, pp. 2 & 7).

We think that the collective peak experiences quoted in Chapter 10 illustrate the nature of society in a golden age in terms of coherence, wakefulness, and efficiency—and the resulting high level of performance and happiness. Such an ideal society may be further illustrated by the following collective peak experience described by Bill Russell,[20] the key player on the Boston Celtics basketball team that won 11 US championships in 13 years. Note that the performance seemed to become so fulfilling in itself that it did not matter to Bill whether they won or lost:

> Every so often a Celtics game would heat up so that it became more than a physical or even mental game, and would be magical. ... When it happened, I could feel my play rise to a new level. It came rarely and would last anywhere from five minutes to a whole quarter, or more. ... It would surround not only me and the other Celtics, but also the players on the other team, and even the referees.
>
> At that special level, all sorts of odd things happened: The game would be in the white heat of competition, and yet somehow I wouldn't feel competitive, which is a miracle in itself. ... The game would move so quickly that every fake, cut, and pass would be surprising, and yet nothing could surprise me. It was almost as if we were playing in slow motion. ... There have been many times in my career when I felt moved or joyful, but these were the moments when I had chills pulsing up and down my spine. ... On the five or ten occasions when the game ended at that special level, I literally did not care who had won. If we lost, I'd still be as free and high as a sky hawk.

$$* \quad * \quad *$$

We've come a long way in this short book, from the integrated brains of world-class athletes, managers, and musicians to creating integration in organizations and society through meditation. But each step is supported by research, and the possibilities for transforming individual experience and all of society excites us. That's why we wrote this book. All the potential is there in our brains. One simply needs to tap into it. We sincerely hope you take the opportunity to do so.

References

Claes, J. (2017, June). *The field paradigm: 20 experiments that can change the world*, 1st ed. www. amazon.com

CNN. (2023). The world just passed a major clean energy milestone | CNN. https://edition.cnn.com/2024/05/08/climate/clean-energy-milestone-ember/. Retrieved September 4, 2024.

Cook-Greuter, S. (1999/2000). *Post autonomous ego development: Its nature and measurement.* PhD dissertation. Harvard Graduate School of Education, Cambridge, Massachusetts, USA. Published by UMI #9933122.

Davies, J. L., & Alexander, C. N. (2005). Alleviating political violence through reducing collective tension: Impact assessment analysis of the Lebanon war. *Journal of Social Behavior and Personality, 17*, 285–338.

Diamandis, P. (2016). https://medium.com/singularityu/why-the-world-is-better-than-you-think-in-10-powerful-charts-9b14b9bbfea8. Retrieved October 12, 2024.

---

[20] Russell & Branch (1979, pp. 155–158).

Diaz, J. (2014). The world is now safer and better than ever and here's the evidence (gizmodo.com). https://gizmodo.com/the-world-is-now-safer-and-better-than-ever-and-heres-t-1651264457. Retrieved July 25, 2024.

Dillbeck, M. C., Landrith, G., III., & Orme-Johnson, D. W. (1981). The transcendental meditation program and crime rate change in a sample of forty-eight cities. *Journal of Crime and Justice, 4*, 25–45.

Dillbeck, M. C., & Cavanaugh, K. (2016, April–June). Societal violence and collective consciousness: Reduction of US homicide and urban violent crime rates. *SAGE Open, 1*–16.

Gates, B. (2018, January 4). Why I decided to edit an Issue of *TIME*. Bill Gates guest edits an issue of TIME | TIME. https://time.com/5086870/bill-gates-guest-editor-time/. Retrieved July 25, 2024.

Global Union of Scientists for Peace. (2024). www.gusp.org. Retrieved September 14, 2024.

Hagelin, J. S. (1987). Is consciousness the unified field? A field theorist's perspective. *Modern Science and Vedic Science, 1*(1), 29–88.

Harung, H. S., & Travis, F. (2016). *Excellence through mind-brain development: The secrets of world-class performers.* Routledge.

Harung, H. S. (1999/2018). *Invincible leadership: Building peak performance organizations by harnessing the unlimited power of consciousness.* MIU Press, Fairfield, Iowa, USA. Original printed version can be ordered from www.miupress.org. Updated 2018 eBook version on www.amazon.com.

Maharishi International University. (1975). *Inauguration of the dawn of the age of enlightenment.* MIU Press Publication Number G 186. Printed in Germany by MIU Press.

Maharishi Mahesh Yogi. (1976). *Creating an ideal society.* MERU Press Publication 1530, Rheinweiler, West Germany.

Moatsos, M. (2021). Global extreme poverty: Present and past since 1820. Published in OECD (2021), *How Was Life? Volume II: New Perspectives on Well-being and Global Inequality since 1820.* OECD Publishing. https://doi.org/10.1787/3d96efc5-en. Retrieved September 6, 2024.

Nader, T. (2024). *Consciousness is all there is: How understanding and experiencing consciousness will transform your life.* Hay House.

Nature. (2023). Editorial, A decades-long decline in extreme poverty has gone into reverse—here's how to fix things. https://www.nature.com/articles/d41586-023-02098-3. Retrieved May 9, 2025.

Orme-Johnson, D. W., Alexander, C. N., Davies, J. L., Chandler, H. M., & Larimore, W. E. (1988). International peace project in the Middle East: The effects of the Maharishi Technology of the unified field. *Journal of Conflict Resolution, 32,* 776–812.

Orme-Johnson, D. W., Cavanaugh, K. L., Dillbeck, M. C., & Goodman, R. S. (2022). Field-effects of consciousness: A seventeen-year study of the effects of group practice of the transcendental meditation and TM-Sidhi Programs on reducing national stress in the United States. *World Journal of Social Science, 9*(2).

Pinker, S. (2019). *Enlightenment now.* Penguin Random House.

Ringen, S. (2017, June). Verden i dag—mye bedre enn den ser ut (World today—much better than it looks) (p. 16). Aftenposten.

Rosling, H. (2018). *Factfulness: Ten reasons we're wrong about the world — and why things are better than you think.* Sceptre.

Russell, W. F., & Branch, T. (1979). *Second wind: The memoirs of an opinionated man.* Random House.

Spivack, B., & Sauders, P. (2020). *An antidote to violence: Evaluating the evidence.* John Hunt Publishing.

Trømborg, E. (2017, June). Dean, Department of Technology, Art, and Design, Oslo Metropolitan University, Norway. Personal communication with Harald S. Harung.

Wilber, K. (2000). *Integral psychology: Consciousness, spirit, psychology, therapy.* Shambhala.

Afterword

World-class performers exhibit many important attitudes and habits that we all can learn from. These qualities naturally characterize the broader vision, greater autonomy, and increased happiness that belong to people with higher mind-brain development. The content of this book has been brought together in a Unified Theory of Performance, which states that the synergy of brain functioning, individual psychology, and frequency of peak experiences together with the social context fundamentally determines an individual's level of performance in any profession or activity.

As you have likely learned from this book, we're passionate about this topic of peak performance. We're convinced that everyone can rise to high levels of performance—and most importantly, lasting happiness. And to achieve this, we think there's much that can be learned from studying world-class performers.

Here are some insights that we've come to, based on our research, some of which are elaborated in our previous book.[1] Peak performers tend to share these qualities:

Qualities of Peak Performers

1. *Use of meditation*. A survey[2] of over 100 billionaires, icons, and world-class performers found that more than 80% of them practiced some form of daily meditation.
2. *Intrinsic motivation* (happiness, passion, autonomy, mastery, self-development, searching for meaning, competing against self, and purpose), not extrinsic motivation (winning, money, power, fame, competing against others).

---

[1] Harung & Travis (2016).

[2] Ferris (2017).

© The Editor(s) (if applicable) and The Author(s), under exclusive license to Springer Nature Switzerland AG 2025
H. S. Harung and F. Travis, *World-Class Brain*, https://doi.org/10.1007/978-3-031-86667-8

3. *Growth orientation*, concerned with continual improvement. The world-class performers know that if they continually improve, they will sooner or later be a peak performer. The Norwegian world-class company Tomra Systems puts it this way: "Better today than yesterday, but not as good as tomorrow."

4. *A focus on mastery and positivity*, not on failure and negativity. The peak-performing handball goalkeeper Heidi Tjugum tells about once having had a bad day. Afterwards she watched videos of only her very best matches. The benefits from this focus on the positive can be explained by the way our brain functions. Every time we think a thought, we strengthen the corresponding underlying brain circuit. Thus, if we think of failure or negative thoughts, we strengthen an *undesirable* brain circuit. In contrast, when we think of mastery, we strengthen a *desirable* brain circuit.

5. *A commitment to the highest.* Our 33 world-class athletes have together won a large number of medals in the Olympic Games, world championships, and European championships: 175 gold medals, 108 silver, and 78 bronze. The fact that they won many more gold medals than silver medals, and many more silver medals than bronze medals, indicates a strong commitment to excellence along the lines of the slogan of the German car maker Mercedes-Benz: "The best, or nothing." Perhaps this commitment is important to consistently perform at a high level?

6. *A focus on prevention and proaction*, not on treatment and reaction. Much of what goes on in today's world is reactive—one tries to solve a problem *after* it has happened. Typically, when a soccer team has not been performing well for some time, the manager is fired, even though research[3] shows that this reactive behavior is expensive and has a negligible positive effect on performance. Or people get sick and then go to the doctor asking for a pill to be healed. In contrast, we observed that many of the top performers were able to prevent problems.

7. *Active use of intuition.* It is a good strategy to train intuition—we can all learn from within ourselves by gradually listening to our gut feeling and delicate mental impulses.

8. *Moral action.* This provides the basis for higher performance, especially in the long term. It's important for high self-esteem and for sleeping well at night.

9. *Taking responsibility* for one's own performance and life. Your manager or anybody else can't make you successful—you have to take responsibility for your own life and performance.

---

[3] Natland (2008).

Characteristics of Individuals with Greater Self-Development

In addition to the above features, peak performers seem to enjoy the mental characteristics that are evident in individuals with higher levels of brain integration and self-development. These characteristics involve a fundamental shift in perspective[4]:

- From *conventional to post-conventional* (ability to think independently)
- From path-following to path-finding
- From control to collaboration
- From short-term to long-term
- From win-lose to win–win interpersonal strategies
- From exclusive to inclusive interpersonal relations
- From reactive to preventive
- From socially derived self-identity to internally derived self-identity

While the conventional person is limited to the conventional perspective, for the post-conventional the post-conventional perspective is primary and the conventional secondary. This means we don't lose any abilities as we develop, we only gain.

The post-conventional person has a broader basis for thinking and acting that will be beneficial for any profession. To illustrate the benefits from higher psychological development, let's consider management. A study[5] of 497 managers in different industries found that 80% of senior managers were at the post-conventional range compared to only about 10% at this level in the general adult population.

Acting as an entrepreneur starting up a new business is a form of leadership that is generally considered more demanding than managing an existing business. These two groups—entrepreneurs and managers—were compared in an interdisciplinary collaboration between neuroscientists and management faculty at MIT. The study[6] found that entrepreneurs, when compared to managers, made their decisions using a more holistic approach that involved creativity and emotions in addition to logic and structured thinking.

The performance benefits resulting from mature self-development are of course not limited to management—such maturity will have benefits in any field of activity. Let's now return to our own research on world-class performers to illustrate this point. First, we[7] used Jane Loevinger's measure of self-development with the athletes and found that the top performers scored significantly higher than the controls. Second, recall that the high performers in sports, management, and music all scored higher than their controls on moral reasoning. Third, a more mature psychology is evident from the above summary of attitudes and habits that we found in the peak performers. Fourth, the higher creativity and post-conventional thinking resulting

---

[4] Harung (1999/2018).

[5] Rooke & Torbert (2005).

[6] Kamenetz (2013).

[7] Harung et al. (2009/2011).

from higher mind-brain development should make it possible to solve the energy and environmental problems that we are facing in the world today.

A Model of How It All Fits Together

This book has presented a number of concepts, such as brain integration, peak experiences, self-development, and collective consciousness. To explain new practical research findings, researchers typically develop new theories. We have therefore developed a model of how it all fits together.

While the current book is oriented more toward a general reader, this model may appeal to those of you who are more theoretically minded.

Previously, performance capacity has been described in terms of psychological factors, notably intelligence. To provide a more comprehensive picture, we have in this book examined the objective measure of brain integration, together with peak experiences and collective consciousness—the social context in which the performer operates.

Our *Unified Theory of Performance*[8] states that the dynamic interplay of brain functioning, individual psychology, and frequency of peak experiences within the ever-changing social and environmental settings fundamentally determines an individual's level of performance in any profession or activity. The first three factors are captured in the Performeasure Assessment. Thus, knowledge of this measure of individual functioning and knowledge of the social context, together provide the information necessary to understand and unfold top-level performance.

Here are the four dimensions of our model:

1. Brain functioning—the level of coherence, relaxed wakefulness, and efficiency of brain functioning. This dimension also includes our genes and our body.
2. Individual psychology—the depth and breadth of mental functioning and feelings as assessed by moral reasoning. Other mental factors that can be assessed are, for example, intelligence, creativity, self-development, and emotional intelligence.
3. Peak experiences—the frequency of peak experiences—the happiest and most fulfilling moments in life. Some of these exhilarating moments are glimpses of higher consciousness, as described in this book.
4. Social context—the level of mind-brain development of the members of the organization and society in which the performer operates.

Figure A.1 illustrates how the four performance dimensions fit into a wholeness. Transcendental Meditation and its advanced practices provide the only procedure that we know of that in one stroke develops all four dimensions of the Unified Theory of Performance, as shown by extensive research

---

[8] Harung & Travis (2016).

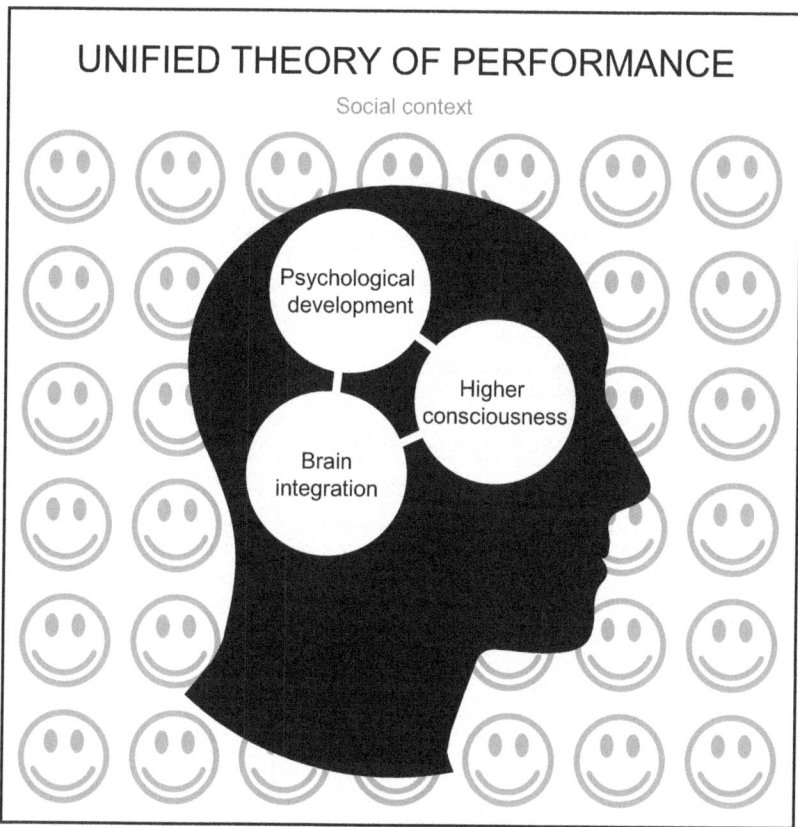

Fig. A.1 Unified theory of performance (The figure illustrates the four dimensions of our Unified Theory of Performance: The three individual dimensions [brain integration, psychological development, and higher consciousness] and the collective dimension—the social context in which the performance takes place)

* * *

This book has brought out how higher brain integration provides the basis for enhanced individual thinking, performing, and achieving—and that everyone has the potential to develop high performance and happiness. To inspire readers to enhance their performance, this afterword has considered some of the important qualities of peak performers, including the enhanced worldview that results from an integrated brain and higher self-development. Finally, our Unified Theory of Performance has integrated the four performance dimensions—brain integration, mature psychology, higher consciousness, and a developed social context—to provide a holistic overview.

We wish you great success in your endeavor to develop higher performance and lasting happiness.

References

Ferris, T. (2017). *Tools of Titans: The tactics, routines, and habits of billionaires, icons, and world-class performers.* Houghton Mifflin Harcourt.

Harung, H., Travis, F., Pensgaard, A. M., Boes, R., Cook-Greuter, S., & Daley, K. (2009). Higher psycho-physiological refinement in world-class Norwegian athletes: Brain measures of performance capacity. *Scandinavian Journal of Medicine and Science in Sports, 21*(1), 32–41. Published online in 2009 and in print in 2011.

Harung, H. S., & Travis, F. (2016). *Excellence through mind-brain development: The secrets of world-class performers.* Routledge.

Harung, H. S. (1999/2018). *Invincible leadership: Building peak performance organizations by harnessing the unlimited power of consciousness.* MIU Press. Original printed version can be ordered from www.miupress.org. Updated 2018 eBook version on www.amazon.com.

Kamenetz, A. (2013, January 14). Brain scans show that entrepreneurs really do think different. *Generation Flux.*

Natland, T. M. (2008). Liten effekt av trenerbyttene (Little effect of coach replacements). Master thesis, Høgskolen i Molde (Molde University College), Molde, Norway.

Rooke, D., & Torbert, W. R. (2005, April). Seven transformations of leadership. *Harvard Business Review.*

If you are happy, you are a high performer

The brains of world-class performers are different from the brains of average performers. No surprise there. But what is surprising is that regardless of whether these top performers are athletes, musicians, or CEOs, their brains share one feature that makes them stand out: More integrated functioning. A world-class brain works in a more coherent, relaxed, wakeful, and efficient way.

World-Class Brain tells the story of these top performers and offers an easy-to-read introduction to the research showing that their brain function is different. This short book also describes other features that these top performers have in common, such as intensely happy and fulfilling peak experiences and a greater moral sense. Readers also learn how they, too, can effortlessly develop greater brain integration.

The manufacturer's authorised representative in the EU is Springer
Nature Customer Service Centre GmbH, Europaplatz 3, 69115 Heidelberg,
Germany. If you have any concerns regarding our products, please
contact ProductSafety@springernature.com

Printed and bound by CPI Group (UK) Ltd, Croydon, CR0 4YY
28/04/2026
02098535-0003